P9-DEP-414

PRAYING *the* ROSARY

MEGAN McKENNA

 A Complete Guide to the World's

Most Popular Form of Prayer

PRAYING *the* ROSARY

DOUBLEDAY | *New York London Toronto Sydney Auckland*

PUBLISHED BY DOUBLEDAY
a division of Random House, Inc.

DOUBLEDAY and the portrayal of an anchor
with a dolphin are registered trademarks
of Random House, Inc.

Book design by Judith Stagnitto Abbate

Grateful acknowledgment is made to the Confraternity
of Christian Doctrine, Inc., for permission to reprint
scripture texts from the New American Bible with New
Testament and Revised Psalms, copyright © 1991, 1986,
1970 by the Confraternity of Christian Doctrine, Inc.,
Washington, DC 10017–1194.

Library of Congress Cataloging-in-Publication Data
McKenna, Megan.
Praying the rosary : a complete guide to the world's
most popular form of prayer / Megan McKenna. —
1st ed.
p. cm.
1. Rosary. 2. Mysteries of the Rosary. 3. Catholic
Church—Prayer-books and devotions—English. I. Title.
BX2163.M355 2004
242'.74—dc22
2003060221

ISBN 0-385-51082-9

Copyright © 2004 by Megan McKenna

All Rights Reserved

PRINTED IN THE UNITED STATES OF AMERICA

May 2004

10   9   8   7   6   5   4   3   2

Contents

With gratitude and love to the Maryknoll missionaries of Bolivia and Peru, and their friends for their hospitality, their dedication to justice and mercy, and their compassionate resistance to injustice and violence. You live the stories that I tell and share your lives with me.

Steve Judd, MM
Jim Madden, MM
Steve DeMott, MM
Jerry McCrane, MM
Larry Kenning, MM
Tom Burns, MM
Maribeth, Steve, and Reiner Bathum
Victor Maqque
Birgit Weiler, MMS
Paul Newpower

ONE

Praying the Rosary with Mary as a Believer

Jesus Christ should be as a book always opened before us from which we are to learn all that is necessary to know.

—CATHERINE MCAULEY

FOR CHRISTIANS in the new millennium, the rosary or prayer beads are familiar aids to prayer. Originally all forms of beads—ropes with knots, cords tightly twisted around one's fingers or wrist or kept hidden in a pocket or under a surplice or apron—served as a reminder to follow the exhortation to pray constantly. Stories are told of the desert fathers and mothers beginning their day by collecting stones, counting them out in sevens, and filling their pockets with them. Then, as the day unfolded and they went about their duties they would finger a stone, pray, and then drop the stone as they walked to their next task; when all the stones were gone, they would stop and once again collect more. These prayers weren't meant to be finished, but were never-ending, a way of praying that was a way of life, drawing the observers daily into a deeper consciousness of being "followers of the way" (the first name for those who followed Jesus Christ).

With the advent of Western monasticism in the fourth century, members of the community were encouraged to learn all one hundred and fifty psalms that were prayed during the seven hours of the Office, the public prayer of the Church meant to draw all of creation—all of time and all the peoples of the world—into an endless prayer from East to West. This was the idea of ringing the world and encircling it, making all one in Christ. Since many could not read or found the task of memorizing the psalms a daunting proposition, they were allowed to substitute the Our Father "Paters" instead, and the recitation of one hundred fifty Our Fathers became a "paternoster." In the Eastern tradition the prayer that was recited was called the "Jesus Prayer" from the Scriptures: "Lord, Jesus Christ, Son of the Living God, have mercy on me, a sinner." This prayer was chanted slowly, carefully, silently or very softly over and over again, filling the one who prayed with a sense of the presence of God everywhere at all times.

John Paul II refers to this tradition of prayer in his recent Apostolic Letter "On the Most Holy Rosary" when he writes: "The Rosary belongs among the finest and most praiseworthy traditions of Christian contemplation. Developed in the West, it is a typically meditative prayer, corresponding in some way to the 'prayer of the heart' or 'Jesus prayer' which took root in the soil of the Christian East." (p. 12, #5)

Just as the Jesus Prayer centered the believer on the person of Christ, so the praying of the Rosary is intended to center the believer on "a commitment to the contemplation of the Christian mystery." (ibid.) The heart and fullness of the Christian mystery is, of course, the person of Jesus Christ, the Word of God made flesh of Mary, the Theotokis (she who bore the Word into the world). Jesus is a singular human being in history and then the Christ of the Word of God (the Scriptures) where this presence of the Risen Lord is given to the Church for all believers to ponder and to incarnate into their own lives now.

John Paul II refers to the Rosary as "a compendium of the Gospel" ("On the Most Holy Rosary," p. 25, #18). And he quotes Paul VI to describe how the Rosary is a Gospel prayer and a Christological prayer.

As a Gospel prayer, centered on the mystery of the redemptive Incarnation, the Rosary is a prayer with a clearly Christological orientation. Its most characteristic element, in fact, the litany-like succession of Hail Marys, becomes in itself an unceasing praise of Christ, who is the ultimate object both of the angel's announcement and the greeting of the mother of John the Baptist: "Blessed is the fruit of your womb" (Luke 1:42). We would go further and say that the succession of Hail Marys constitutes the warp on which is woven the contemplation of the mysteries. The Jesus that each Hail Mary recalls is the same Jesus whom the succession of mysteries proposes to us now as the Son of God, now as the Son of the Virgin. (#28 Apostolic Exhortation *Marials Cultus* [February 2, 1974], 46: AAS 6 [1974], 155)

Again, there is that image of the loom, and the warp describing how the singular thread of the Hail Marys is meant to disappear into the other threads, the mysteries of the Word of God in the Scriptures. Always the unifying element is the Word of God. Again John Paul II writes: "The Rosary is also a path of proclamation and increasing knowledge, in which the mystery of Christ is presented again and again at different levels of the Christian experience. Its form is that of a prayerful and contemplative presentation, capable of forming Christians according to the heart of Christ." (p. 23, #17)

It is with this in mind that John Paul II decided to add to the traditional mysteries of the Rosary. As the Rosary developed in the Middle Ages, much of the core of the Scriptures, the life and teachings of Jesus, was omitted, with concentration on his birth, and sufferings, death, and resurrection. Since many could not read, emphasis was placed upon events and moments that had been described in the Gospels while neglecting the teachings, parables, and prayers of Jesus. What was left out was the heart of the Good News, "the mysteries of Christ's public ministry between his Baptism and his passion." (p. 26, #19) Even with the insertion of these five new mysteries of light, or luminous mysteries, only a tiny portion of the Word of God in the Gospels is highlighted for reflection. The five mysteries of light are turning points, or large theological concepts that are found fleshed out in the Gospels. They are, as it were, jumping-off places, catalysts for entering into the depths of the Word of God in the Scriptures. The moments of light that have been singled out are: I. Jesus' baptism in the Jordan, 2. his self-manifestation at the wedding of Cana; 3. his proclamation of the Kingdom of God, with his call to conversion, 4. his transfiguration; and finally, 5. his institution of the Eucharist, as the sacramental expression of the Paschal Mystery. RVM*, "Each of these mysteries is a revelation of the Kingdom now present in the very person of Jesus." (pp. 28–29, #21)

In some ways the inclusion of these five luminous mysteries is an attempt to introduce major themes of the

---

* Throughout, RVM refers to the Apostolic letter *Rosarium Virginis Mariae* of the Supreme Pontiff John Paul II to the Bishops, Clergy, and Faithful on the Most Holy Rosary, October 16, 2002.

entire Gospels. The focus is to be on Jesus and only secondarily on Mary as believer, who with us seeks to follow the commands of Jesus, walking in his way, his truth and life, toward the Father, in the power of the Spirit. John Paul II explains how Mary is "found" in these mysteries.

> In these mysteries, apart from the miracle of Cana, the presence of Mary remains in the background. The Gospels make only the briefest reference to her occasional presence at one moment or other during the preaching of Jesus (cf. Mark 3:31–35; John 2:12), and they give no indication that she was present at the Last Supper and the institution of the Eucharist. Yet the role she assumed at Cana in some way accompanies Christ throughout his ministry. The revelation made directly by the Father at the Baptism in the Jordan and echoed by John the Baptist is placed upon Mary's lips at Cana, and it becomes the great maternal counsel which Mary addresses to the Church of every age: "Do whatever he tells you" (John 2:5). This counsel is a fitting introduction to the words and signs of Christ's public ministry and it forms the Marian foundation of all the "mysteries of light." (RVM, p. 30, #21)

Again, this command is directed to us, summoning us to obey the Word of God as found in the Scriptures, to concentrate on focusing our attention on what Jesus is doing and how he is revealing what the kingdom looks like now, in his presence on earth.

John Paul II seeks in his Apostolic Letter to help the Church to "rediscover the age-old tradition of the recitation of the Rosary" in the same light as his exhortation to rediscover the Liturgy of the Hours, in his letter *"Novo Millennio Ineunte,"* asking parish communities and groups to make the Office a part of their daily life. With the addition of the mysteries of light, the Pope seeks to infuse new life into this devotion, calling for renewed consciousness of the need to "pray always and not lose heart" (Luke 13:1) and to situate all prayer in the context of the Word of God, the Scriptures. As Thérèse of Lisieux said in her writings: ". . . it is especially the Gospels which sustain me during my hours of prayer, for in them I find what is necessary for my poor little soul. I am constantly discovering in them new lights, hidden and mysterious meanings." (Quoted in "On Reading with Abandonment," Pat Hall, *Living Prayer,* September/ October 1994, pp. 13–17)

As with all devotions, the five mysteries' intent is to lead toward a deeper appreciation of and participation in the Liturgy of the Word and the Eucharist. Private and devotional communal prayer are to be practiced as the necessary basis for delving ever more deeply into the sources of our Christian life: the Word of God in the Scriptures, the Liturgy of the Eucharist, and the sacraments. The recitation of the Rosary with contemplative reflection on the mysteries of the gospel must invariably lead to an intimate reading, study, and love of the Word of God itself. As John Paul reminds us, as we pray the Rosary, it must be prayed with concentration, attentiveness, and with an attitude of conversion of heart and life, or it is an empty, run-on prayer. He writes:

> The Rosary, precisely because it starts with Mary's own experience, is an exquisitely contemplative prayer. Without this contemplative dimension, it would lose its meaning, as Pope Paul VI clearly pointed out: "Without contemplation, the Rosary is a body without a soul, and its recitation runs the risk of becoming a mechanical repetition of formulas, in violation of the admonition of Christ: 'In praying do not heap up empty phrases as the Gentiles do; for they think they will be heard for their many words' (Matthew 6:7). By its nature the recitation of the Rosary calls for a quiet rhythm and a lingering pace, helping the individual to meditate on the mysteries of the Lord's life as seen through the eyes of her who was closest to the Lord. In this way the unfathomable riches of these mysteries are disclosed." (Apostolic Exhortation *Marialis Cultus* [February 2, 1974], 47: AAS [1974], 156 in JPII [p. 17, #12])

For these reasons, each of the reflections presented in this book on the twenty mysteries of Christ's life as contemplated in the Rosary prayer will begin with portions of the Scriptures to be read and reflected upon prior to the actual recitation. And it is hoped that reflection upon these short pieces of the Word of God will lead those who pray the Rosary to use the Scriptures as their essential and basic prayer, alone and in community, along with the

Liturgy of the Eucharist, and to see the Word as primary to the Christian life of prayer.

THE ROSARY AS A PRAYER FOR PEACE

"The Rosary is by its nature a prayer for peace,
since it consists in the contemplation of Christ,
the Prince of Peace, the one who is 'our peace.' "

—EPHESIANS 2:14; P. 50, #40

At the very beginning of his Apostolic Letter on the Rosary, John Paul II writes that the Rosary needs to be prayed in these times "first of all, . . . to implore from God the gift of peace." (p. 12, #6) This millennium began with acts of terrorism, violence, and bloodshed, and has continued to escalate into worldwide nationalistic and religious confrontations that threaten to engulf humankind in a future of fear. On January 13, 2003, the Pope met with ambassadors of the world at the Vatican to categorically state that there cannot be another war. He spoke forcibly, stressing both the teaching of the Church and of the United Nations. His points situate any prayer in the context of harsh and demanding realities that surround all peoples of the earth.

> After referring to "the feeling of fear which often dwells in the hearts of our contemporaries," and the "insidious terrorism capable of striking at any

time anywhere," as well as "the unresolved problem of the Middle East," the Pope today ex-
claimed: "No to war! War is not always inevitable.
It is always a defeat for humanity."

On the contrary, "international law, honest
dialogue, solidarity between states, the noble exercise of diplomacy: These are the methods worthy of individuals and nations in resolving their
differences. I say this as I think of those who still
place their trust in nuclear weapons and of the all-
too-numerous conflicts which continue to hold
hostage our brothers and sisters in humanity."

Adamantly, he continued teaching, and exhorting the
ambassadors:

And what are we to say of the threat of war which
could strike the people of Iraq, the land of the
prophets, a people already sorely tried by more
than 12 years of embargo? War is never just another means that one can choose to employ for
settling differences between nations. . . . The
solution will never be imposed by recourse to terrorism or armed conflict, as if military victories
could be the solution. (Zenit, Vatican City,
January 13, 2003; State of the World, According
to John Paul II)

As part of this address, John Paul cried out: "No to
Death! No to Selfishness! No to War!" It is in light of

these words to the ambassadors of the world community that his words in the Apostolic Letter on the Rosary must be read and taken to heart: "Consequently, one cannot recite the Rosary without feeling caught up in a clear commitment to advancing peace, especially in the land of Jesus, still so sorely afflicted and so close to the heart of every Christian." (p. 12, #6) This theme is returned to again and again in the letter, calling everyone who prays the Rosary to engage in the active work of justice, care for the poor, dialogue, nonviolent conflict negotiation, demand for universal law, and resistance to the idea of the use of weapons and military force as inevitable or even to be considered, except as an extreme possibility after every other option has been exhausted. As he addresses all believers at the end of the letter, he writes specifically of becoming peacemakers as a necessity for all who believe the Word of God and pray the Rosary.

> In a word, by focusing our eyes on Christ, the Rosary also makes us peacemakers in the world. By its nature as an insistent choral petition in harmony with Christ's invitation to "pray ceaselessly" (Luke 18:1), the Rosary allows us to hope that, even today, the difficult "battle" for peace can be won. Far from offering an escape from the problems of the world, the Rosary obliges us to see them with responsible and generous eyes, and obtains for us the strength to face them with the certainty of God's help and the intention of

bearing witness in every situation to "love, which binds everything together in perfect harmony." (Colossians 3:14) (pp. 50–51, #40)

Alongside this call to participate in the transformation of the world into the kingdom of peace with justice comes the explanation of the possible effects of the Rosary on the Church communities of parish and family. The Pope reminds believers that the Rosary in the past often brought families closer together. And this devotion to the Rosary is linked to the necessity of saying the Liturgy of the Hours in small communities and parishes so that they complement each other as two paths of Christian contemplation. Praying together in public, believers, "in turning their eyes towards Jesus, also regain the ability to look one another in the eye, to communicate, to show solidarity, to forgive one another and to see their covenant of love renewed in the Spirit of God." (RVM, p. 51, #41)

The theologian Karl Barth wrote, "To clasp one's hands in prayer is the beginning of an uprising against the disorder of the world." But it is only the beginning of a way of life that allows believers to resist evil and practice virtue steadfastly as a personal endeavor and, as a community, to witness to the gospel in their ethics and public behaviors. Bernard of Clairvaux wrote, "While offering up the sacrifice of praise . . . let us make every endeavor to put meaning into our observance, to fill the meaning with love, our love with joy and our joy with realism; let that realism be tempered with humility and our humility buoyant with liberty." The person of Jesus Christ, the Word of God, is the ultimate source of all virtue and holiness, and it is in our actions, our decisions, and our associations with others that our belief in Him is practiced and attested to, rather than any statement of theology or protestation of belief. It is in putting our reputations, what we hold dear, and our very lives on the line that we stand up for what we believe and obey the Word of God.

Simone Weil, in the past century, put this reality in terms that cannot be refuted:

> Christ does not save all those who say to Him, "Lord, Lord." But he saves all those who out of a pure heart give a piece of bread to a starving man, without thinking about Him the least little bit. And these, when He thanks them, reply: "Lord, when did we feed thee?" An atheist and an infidel, capable of pure compassion, are as close to God as is a Christian, and consequently know Him equally well, although their knowledge is expressed in other words, or remains unspoken. For "God is Love."

If we are to "take up the Rosary" once again as part of our tradition, we must again "take up our cross" and "take the Word of God into our hearts" along with the poor, the victims of injustice and violence. In fact, we must stretch our hearts to take the whole world within, holding all peoples, especially our enemies, with tender regard just as our God—the Trinity of the Father, the Son, and the Spirit—holds all of us securely, strongly, and freely.

MARY AS A BELIEVER AND DISCIPLE IN THE SCRIPTURES

"She is the loom on which God wove his design."

—PROCLUS OF CONSTANTINOPLE

This phrase was used to describe Mary—or Myriam, as she would have been called in Hebrew, after Miriam, the prophetess and leader of song at the Red Sea, who was the sister of Moses. It was she who saved her brother by placing him in a basket of reeds and sending it downstream, where it would be found by Pharaoh's daugher, Bithia. And it was probably she who suggested to the Egyptian princess that she knew a Hebrew woman-slave who would nurse the child. It was Miriam who saved Moses's life so that he could grow up to be the liberator and the lawgiver of the people Israel. There are so many women named Mary, so many Myriams in the Gospels, that we often forget it was the hope and prayer of every Jewish woman that she would be the mother of the one who would set Israel free once again and that her child would be the one who would be called the Son of Justice and Peace, often referred to as the Messiah. Mary's history and tradition were, from the very beginning, closely related to the Word of Yahweh, who bent down to hear the cries of his people in bondage and then sent Moses to save his people and call them out of slavery and into a future as a covenanted people belonging to God alone. Every woman in Israel fervently hoped to be bound up with the liberation of her people and play a pivotal role in fulfilling God's Word, making Israel the light to all the other nations.

Who is this woman Mary, the mother of Jesus, the Word of God in the Scriptures? Perhaps a story from one of the Native American traditions can shed light on who she is, both as a Jew, a believer, a disciple, and a member of her community. The story is from the Abenaki tribe, from upstate New York and the New England area as it extends into eastern Canada. This version, I heard from an Abenaki storyteller, Joseph Bruchac, who is Abenaki Indian and Polish by descent. I heard it many years ago and it has stayed with me, making me think over and over again, dig more deeply into my own tradition of Christianity, ponder the similarities with his traditions, and wonder at the depth of shared belief and practice. This is the way I tell it now, most often as introductory material in talking about Mary, as believer and disciple among all the children of God.

Once upon a time, there lived four friends. They had grown up together, lived close by one another, played and hunted and learned their skills as warriors and married and had children, sharing so much in common. And they still gathered together on winter evenings and told the old stories they had heard as children, and their dreams and hopes. In fact, night after night, winter after winter, the talk always came back to the same topic. They had dreamed as children and young men of going on a journey together, in search of the Great Spirit to ask of him a favor, a gift, and then return home to share that with others. But they had never gone and it was all they talked about. Finally, it was their wives who got together and decided it was time for them to stop talking and go on that journey. The wives prepared for the time away, laying in extra food, hides, and skins, and made sure that they had everything they needed for an extended stay without their husbands. The men worked hard and it was time for them to go. There were farewells filled with the paradox of joy for the journey long awaited and sadness at leaving their wives and children, their village, and their lives behind them. But they had wanted to do this their whole life long. And so they went their way.

They paddled their canoes all day, resting that night, and again a second day. By the third day they had gone farther from their village than any of them had been before. It was new territory. They were excited and a bit fearful but paddled on. They heard a great roaring and wondered if they were getting close to the home of the Great Spirit, Gitchie Manitou. The waters were rough, the currents quick, and they were fighting to keep control of their canoes when all of a sudden, they saw where they were headed: rushing waters, great rocks, and then—over a mighty falls! In a flash they knew why no one had ever returned from their journeys to find the Great Spirit. And they went sailing out over the falls and fell thousands of feet into the roaring waters below.

When they awoke it was dark and they found themselves in a cave. At first they thought they were dead and in the land of the spirits. They were dressed in fresh deerskins, beautiful clothing, and they were warm and dry. And then they were served, by beautiful young men and women, food and drink that were more delicious than anything they had ever tasted. There was music, singing, dancing, and storytelling, and they looked at one another and tried to remember everything so that, if they got back home, they could share it with their people. And then they noticed an ancient elder over in the corner whom all the people deferred to with reverence. He beckoned to them and they rose, and sat around him in a circle. They knew, sitting in the silence, that this was the One they had sought. This One was the Great Spirit. He smoked his pipe slowly, watching them and looking deeply into each one of them in turn. Then he spoke solemnly and welcomed them to his home along the river, under the great falls called Niagara. They were his guests for the evening, and in the morning they would be given all they needed for their journey home. But now it was time for them to ask for what they wanted, a gift to take with them, for that was the reason they had come looking for him.

He looked at the first man, who knew exactly what he

wanted. He had thought of this moment all his life. He said, "I want the gift of living longer than anyone else." The others looked at him, surprised, but he went on to explain: "Among our people there is a great need for wisdom, and wisdom is most often obtained by long life, experience, and acquired knowledge. That is what I want." The Great Spirit looked at him, nodded, and picked up a deerskin bag. He blew his breath into it, pulled the strings tight, and gave it to the man with the words: "Do not open this until you get home and are in the presence of your loved ones and all the people." And he turned to the next man. He spoke quickly, knowing exactly what he wanted as his gift: "I want to be taller than anyone else in my tribe." The others were startled once again—why that gift? But he went on to explain: "Among our people, a leader usually stands tall, towering above the others. I am very short and no one thinks that I could be a leader, but I want to lead my people to their destiny." The Great Spirit looked at him, nodded, and picked up a deerskin bag. He blew his breath into it, pulled the strings tight, and gave it to him with the words: "Do not open this until you get home and are in the presence of your loved ones and all the people."

He looked toward the third man, who spoke confidently: "I want to have more than anyone else in my tribe." Then he immediately realized that the request must sound selfish, and he went on to explain. "In our tribe, it is the custom to practice giveaways, making sure that all are taken care of and all have what they need, especially if they are old, or poor, or ill, or orphans and widows. I want to be able to give to all of them and make sure that there is no one in need." The Great Spirit looked at him, nodded, and picked up a deerskin bag. He blew his breath into it, pulled the strings tight, and gave it to him with the words: "Do not open this until you get home and are in the presence of your loved ones and all the people." And then it was the last man's turn. The Great Spirit turned and looked and him, and the man was distraught. After a moment he spoke: "I don't know what I want. I have thought of this all my life and I don't know what is needed." The Great Spirit looked at him long and then said, "What if I give you a gift of my choosing?" The man nodded gratefully. So the Great Spirit took a deerskin bag, blew his breath into it, pulled the strings tight, and gave it to him with the words: "Do not open this until you get home and are in the presence of your loved ones and all the people." And the man took his bag, as had the others, holding it close to his heart. They listened to the music, and the stories, and soon fell into a deep, heavy sleep. When they awoke the next morning they found themselves in their canoes, once again upon the waters and heading back to their village.

They looked at one another in amazement and word-lessly started to paddle for home as fast as they could. Now the only important thing was to get home. They raced, paddling all day, all night, stopping only when they could not go any farther, drifting in their canoes, their paddles on their knees. On the second day, one of the men, the one who wanted to live longer than any one else, pulled out ahead and disappeared around a bend in the river. Out of sight, he stopped and took out his bag, thinking to himself, It will be fine if I just take a peek inside and see what is in here. He opened the bag and *swoosh . . .* the Great Spirit's breath was released and immediately the man became a great, heavy stone, sinking through the canoe and down into the depths of the river. And, they say, he has lived longer than anyone in his tribe. Just then, the second man came around the bend of the river ahead of the other two and slowed his pace, taking out his bag. He been thinking to himself too: I'll just open the bag a little bit and see what's in there. So he pulled the strings and the Great Spirit's breath was released and immediately the man shot up, becoming a great, tall tree with its roots plunging through the bottom of the canoe, deep into the soil at the bottom of the river. And they say he is taller than anyone in his tribe still.

The other two paddled past the tree, not remembering a great tree in the middle of the river, but not thinking much about it. They were intent on getting home and wondered how the other two had gotten so far ahead of them. The third man now pulled ahead and paddled to the end of a small outcrop of land, at the far end of the village, away from anyone's sight. He'd planned this with his wife from the very beginning. She would be waiting for him there, and as he hoped, there she was on the end of the spit of land. He pulled up and she jumped into the canoe. They floated a ways out into deeper water and she excitedly asked him what had happened. He blurted out some of the story and got immediately to the part about getting the gift. "Did you ask for more than everyone else?" "Yes" he answered and together they opened the bag. The Great Spirit's breath was released and suddenly their canoe was filled with hides, skins, kettles, brass, arrowheads, feathers, game, corn, seed, and it just kept piling up. Before they could do anything, the canoe sank with the weight and the two of them went down with all their new possessions and they drowned. They still are the ones with more things than anyone else in the village.

The last man paddled as quickly as he could toward the village, near exhaustion, wondering where the others were. The word went up and they were waiting for him as he drew his canoe up on the shore. He was embraced by his wife and children, his parents and relations, while all the members of the tribe from the elders to the newborn gathered around. They drew him into a tepee, fed him, and let him rest for a while. Then later in the evening all gathered in the tent to listen to his story and find out what had happened to him while he was gone on his journey. He was told that none of his three friends had yet returned. He was the only one who had made it home.

He began and told them of the journey, the days away and the new territory and the great falls and how they could not stop and went over, thinking they would die. He told them about waking up under the falls in the home of the Great Spirit, of the food and the beautiful people and the music, the songs and the stories he heard.

And then he spoke of the Great Spirit smoking the pipe of peace, and of being his guests and the gifts. He told of the other three men and their requests and how they had been given deerskin bags with the Great Spirit's breath held inside and told not to open their gifts until they were home with their loved ones and the rest of the tribe. And then he told them of his hesitation and not knowing what to ask for and the Great Spirit's suggestion that he himself choose the gift he would give to him. And he too was given the Great Spirit's breath in the deerskin bag and told not to open it. He told of the trip back and showed them the bag. There was a great silence and many deep breaths and sighs as he opened his bag. The Great Spirit's breath was released but when he looked into the bag, he found that it was empty! There was nothing in the bag! He sat stunned and silent, disappointed, fearful, confused, remembering all that had happened, and dug deep into his heart wondering what this might mean, pondering all these things in his heart. The people all sat there for many hours, and then one by one they left to go to their own homes, until only his wife remained with him in the silence.

Life went on in the village, and often the people would see him sitting under a tree, or inside his tepee, or down by the river, holding his bag close to his heart, his eyes open or closed, and his body silent, straining, listening to all around and within him, saying nothing. He would carefully open the bag that had held the Great Spirit's breath, and sit, pondering all these things in his heart. Then one day, the elders came to him, asking his help and opinion. There had been many months without rain, and the crops were wilting and dying. This was the second year in a row where they would lose all their food. Did he know what to do? He sat, pondering their question for many hours, into the night, holding his bag from the Great Spirit, and in the morning he came to them with the idea of building a series of canals that would bring the water from the Great River to the fields. It was hard work but the crops survived, and from that year on they did not have to depend upon just the rains for their harvest. Months went by and the elders came to him again. This time there was a strange sickness in the camps that spared no one—the old, the young, or the women giving birth. Did he know what it was or how to stop its walk of death? Again, for many days and nights he sat with his deerskin bag and pondered their question and his people's pain. Finally he rose and asked for the shamans, the medicine women, to walk with him in the woods. He asked them what certain roots and leaves were used for and how they both helped and hindered when they were used. And together they came up with a tea for all the people to drink. It was bitter, but there were no more deaths in the village, and with other herbs the people recovered.

This was how it happened: They would come to him whenever there was a need among the people, or they suffered, or there was dissension in the camps or arguments among the clans. And he would sit with his deerskin bag and ponder all these things in his heart, digging deep into memory, story, music, and his people's pain until he knew what to do. The people came to rely on him and they made him their chief, obeying his counsel, and for many decades there was peace among the people who followed him. They say his name was Hiawatha and that he was favored by the Great Spirit, and that as long as they sat together and pondered these things with the deerskin bag, there was always a way of hope, a way to follow, and the people prospered and dwelled in peace. That is what they say when they tell this story, called "Digging Deep."

This story says so much about the Great Spirit, about gifts and being favored, about community and prayer, about gifts given for the people, about obedience and openness to serve others. And it speaks reams about contemplation, of "pondering all these things in your heart," of reflecting on the Great Spirit's words and living in the presence of the Great Spirit's breath, which renews, responds, gives, heals, and makes meaning, redeeming all situations and relationships among the people. This is in a very true sense a story about Mary and her life once the Spirit of God came upon her. But it is also a story about all of our lives when the Spirit of God has come upon us in our baptisms of water and the spirit. And then we learn to obey and to ponder all these things, attempting to see our lives in light of the Word of the Gospels. This image, perhaps more than any other, can help us to look at Mary, as believer, as disciple, as healer, as one who prays and listens to the community and who reflects upon the Word, as we too are called to do with her.

There are only a few stories about Mary in the Gospels, and she lives and has meaning only in relation to the Word made flesh revealed in the Scriptures. She is barely mentioned in Mark, except for a reference found in all the Synoptic Gospels (Mark, Matthew, and Luke). This is the incident in which Jesus' relatives come to him while he is teaching his disciples, and when he is told about their presence outside, waiting for him, he says: "Who is my mother, my brother and my sister? Anyone who hears the Word of my Father and obeys it is mother, brother and sister to me." (Mark 3:31, Matthew 12:48) In Matthew's gospel she is seen and mentioned only in relation to her child, described in the first chapters as "This is how Jesus Christ was born. Mary his mother . . ." And the other references are similar: "Take the child and his mother," the command again and again from the angel to Joseph. She has no other existence than that of birthing the Word into the world.

In Luke she appears only in the first three chapters, as betrothed to a man of the house of David, as the obedient servant accepting the good news of the Incarnation, giving birth and then living with whom her child might be for others. She is described twice as "pondering all these things in her heart," once after the shepherds come to visit and tell of the song of the angels in the night, and in the same segment of the gospel when the prophet Simeon tells her that a "sword will pierce her own heart because this child is a sign of contradiction for his own people and will be the cause of the rise and fall of many in the house of Israel." She is mentioned once again, when

Jesus goes down with her and Joseph from Jerusalem after they have lost him in the temple. Mary, in Luke's
gospel, is the image or the icon of the believer in the gentile community who hears the gospel, responds, and takes
it to heart, pondering this power of the Spirit and Word
of God in her own life. She grows in knowledge and understanding and sings the praises of God among the people, as she does in the song of the Magnificat. She is a
prophet announcing the coming justice of God. She is
the one who first believed and brought the Word to bear
flesh in the world, and she is also the first disciple who
struggles to understand who this child will grow up to be.
This is the last glimpse we have of her in Luke, where she
is described as "pondering all these things in her heart."
Then, the gospel turns toward the grown man Jesus as he
walks out of the desert and into the synagogue in his
hometown of Nazareth, announcing the presence of the
Kingdom of God in his own person and presence. Luke
presents Mary as the one who ponders all these things
throughout the rest of her life. She lives contemplatively,
cherishing all that happens, listening to others' stories,
and pondering the entire gospel as she seeks to believe in
the Word of God made flesh in Jesus, who brings healing
and hope, good news to the poor, and the power of God
to bear upon injustice and violence in the world. She is
mentioned only once again in Luke, in the first chapter
of the Acts of the Apostles, where she is named among the
other men and women praying and waiting for the coming of the Spirit upon the fledgling church at Pentecost.

Here she is last seen as a believer among believers, waiting once again on the coming of the Spirit into the world, into history, and into the hearts of believers who obey his word.

In the Gospel of John we are given two glimpses of her, now called "woman." She is found only in chapters two and nineteen, where she is the icon of the Church, first at the wedding feast of Cana, and then as she stands with the other named disciples, young John, Mary of Magdala, and her own sister, Mary of Cleopas. Here in these places, at a wedding feast and at the place of crucifixion, are where the Church stands and should always be found: at ease in the back rooms of those who are the servants of the kingdom of justice, of the poor, and of peace, as often sung of in Isaiah's writings, and standing witness, even silently, at the side of those who suffer unjustly and violently at the hands of other human beings. Her last words spoken in all of the Scriptures must be taken to heart as most descriptive of her own life, belief, and meaning: "Do whatever he tells you!" (John 2) All else can be construed as superficial, artificial, contrived, or even in opposition to the Word of God made flesh in her womb, who is Jesus the Son of God among us.

This is all we see and know of her. She is a woman of few words and one song and a lifetime of pondering "all these things in her heart." "All these things" are the mysteries of her child, in words, actions, presence, and demands in the world. And this child, this man Jesus, is first Son of the Father, Son of God, Word of God made flesh, and only then her child, who belongs to all the people of God from the beginning of the covenant. And his own words reveal that he belongs with greater intimacy to all those who are his disciples, who obey and take to heart his Father's words, then to his mother. To those who bear the word of his Father into the world—these are known as mother, brother, and sister, in the grace and favor of the Spirit.

This woman is loved, cherished, ignored, leaned upon, dismissed, theologized about, held up as a model, and used as criteria for all other women in some cultures. She is seen as impossible to imitate, used as a crutch, a club, and sometimes as an alternative to all that is found in the actual Scriptures. There are few and short though potent pieces of scripture that place her in perspective to the Word and Person of the Scriptures, Jesus, the Son of Man, the Son of Justice, the Son of God made human. There is an anonymous saying that captures in a line or two what perhaps she herself might think of what she has been made and become in two thousand years of history, devotion, and distortion: "What have you done to me? What have you made of me? I cannot find myself in the woman you want me to be . . . Haloed, alone . . . marble and stone. Safe, gentle, holy Mary."

These are startling words, but indicative of the range of perceptions that describe a simple woman who would never have imagined herself in any of the devotions, guises, artwork, and positions of power that she now finds herself, as queen, or as one who is distant and other than all others. And sometimes she is treated apart from the Scriptures and, even on occasion, in opposition to the words of the Scriptures and her own words in the Gospels.

These small pieces, gleanings of the scripture passages where she is mentioned, are crucial to any understanding of who this woman Mary actually was and is today for believers. Someone once said that wisdom is found in the details. What do we know of her? She was a Jew, which meant that she lived on the psalm prayers of her tradition. There are one hundred fifty of them that were prayed daily, weekly, in every area of life: walking, working, before and after rising and upon going to sleep; in times of distress, confusion, persecution, hardship, joy, comfort, dryness, and darkness, as well as in times of light, community festivals, and worship. She saw her life and the life of her people, the Israelites, through the lens of weekly Sabbath observance and the readings of the Torah. But even more to the point, she lived on hope, a hope that meant the coming of justice for the poor, for the powerless in the world, and for those faithful to the covenant. She would have known these prayers and whole segments of the words and promises of the prophets by heart, as well as large portions of the law by recitation and constant practice. And she would have lived on the hope that she might give birth to the long-awaited one, who would, like her namesake of old, Miriam, draw forth from the waters, the one who would be Savior to the people once again.

She was a singer, a poet, and a prophetess who prayed passionately, using the ancient texts of her people. She was about announcing justice coming, scattering the proud in their conceit, and shattering their self-righteous hearts, shouting out that the mighty would be taken down from their thrones and the lowly (probably all the people she ever knew) would be lifted up. She dreamed of the day of judgment, when the rich would be exposed as empty-hearted and sent away empty-handed. And then she would be a part of the remnant feeding the poor and the hungry with the feast of a future where there was enough to share among all in need. And intimacy with God would be given to the faithful believers as graciously and generously as peace with justice would be given to all the peoples of the earth. In all these prayers sung with such belief, she was a daughter of her people, of the covenant, and of obedience to the God of Israel.

In other cultures she is the one who goes before the face of the Lord, preparing the people for the Word made flesh to be born among them. She is fondly called La Morenita, the Virgin of Guadalupe in Mexico. This Mary is the woman of the land. She is sister to the poor and the mother of compassion and healing for all those who live on the edges of life, walking the roads on the outskirts of the cities, living in slums, *favelas,* tenements, and the neighborhoods no one wants to ever get caught having to raise their children in. She is barefoot upon the earth; her presence causes roses to bloom in December and the birds to sing wildly and the land to bring forth its seed and bread for those desperate for daily sustenance (still more than 85 percent of the earth) and freedom. She can be a spider, as in the Native American tradition, who follows a trail home bringing light to the people, silent, unnoticed, so small and so able to steal the light from those who will not share it with others. She is the symbol of the small of the earth, inconsequential except to God, found with all those who live faithfully in situations of darkness, despair, lack, and need, yet powerful in their very weakness and numbers.

She is the Black Madonna, her face slashed in violence and rage, who sees and is witness to all the horror men and women are capable of inflicting upon one another in war, murder, torture. She is caught up with the civilians of all nations eating one another alive, sending thousands into exile, driving the weakest of the earth into fear and insecurity, while the earth is pillaged and left a desolate, uninhabitable wasteland. In Asian countries she is called Kuan Yin, or Kannon, "the one who hears all cries," and with many arms she reaches out in pity and compassion to all seeking help, listening to the sorrows of the world. As one Japanese poet said: "She is a mother. She has born a child in the midst of tenderness and violence. And I remember that whenever I look at my own wife and child, conscious of their own fragility and indescribable beauty. And she becomes every woman, child, and man who hopes for a just life."

She was just a poor woman like so many others of any backwater village in any poor nation, in an occupied territory, who lived in hope of a life of dignity, freedom, and peace with her neighbors, her relations, and her land. Today she could have lived in the West Bank of Palestine, a thickly veiled woman hidden in a burkah, wailing as she watched another house destroyed needlessly in mindless, violent retaliation for other acts of violence, another victim among thousands. She still lives among us. Now she can be found in an endless litany of places filled with agony and hate: Afghanistan, Iraq, Somalia, the southern islands of the Philippines, Sierra Leone, the mountains of Colombia, the villages of Peru, the refugee camps of West Timor, Bosnia, every place where war reigns instead of her son's kingdom of peace with justice and care for the poor. She is found in every mother, sister, wife, daughter, every human being who grieves the death of the innocent, who buries a child, who knows fear, insecurity, and torture at the hands of others, and fears for the lives and souls of those she loves.

She was anyone and everyone who, once aware of being in the presence of the holy, found her life transfigured by grace and spirit into a life bound to others in suffering, birth, death, and resurrection. She knew she was favored and blessed by God. She was grateful for God's notice of her and shouted out to anyone who would take her words to heart that they too could be so honored by God and they too could bring the Word into the world and be the servant of all those who cry out in their pain for God's touch, God's compassion and justice in their worlds. She believed, but she believed on behalf of and with all her people, with all people still, and calls us to believe with her, on behalf of the earth and all God's children in this generation.

Proclus of Constantinople described her as "the loom on which God wove his design . . ." The loom still stands, strung with threads bright with color and shades of light and dark, and there is still much weaving to be done in our lives and in the world. We, by our baptisms, are also called to stand and be the looms where God's Spirit and Word weave the designs that will create a world that visibly belongs to God; a world careful of the poor, intent on justice, steeped in peace and honoring God, who is the Father of Jesus and the Father of all of us born on this earth. And as always there is singing, as the design becomes visible to others.

> *Let us sing with this woman, so free and so strong*
> *Who embraces the lowly, comforting those who mourn.*
> *Who summons wine for the poor by her meek command;*
> *And gathers all people to stand hand in hand.*
> *Come, let us cry justice and cause spring to be born*
> *As we share her hope with all people, and continue her song.*

How to Pray the Rosary

TWO

THE WAY IT IS

There's a thread you follow. It goes among
*   things that change. But it doesn't*
*   change.*
People wonder about what you are
*   pursuing.*
You have to explain about the thread.
But it is hard for others to see.
While you hold it you can't get lost.
Tragedies happen; people get hurt or die;
*   and you suffer and get old.*
Nothing you do can stop time's unfolding.
You don't ever let go of the thread.

> —WILLIAM STAFFORD,
> FROM *EARLY MORNING:*
> *REMEMBERING MY FATHER*
> BY KIM STAFFORD
> (MINNEAPOLIS:
> GRAYWOLF PRESS, 2002)

THERE IS no right way to pray the Rosary. It is like a thread that runs through our lives. The thread is not so much the beads themselves, or even the specific prayers such as the Hail Mary, the Our Father, and the Doxology, that form the actual pattern of the Rosary, but it is the Word of God, the scripture, that is the thread, tied on one end to us and the other end to God. We are bound in the humanity and divinity of Jesus to God and to each other. And it is seeded deep in our nature as human beings to pray. Harriet Beecher Stowe once wrote, "Prayer is a long rope with a strong hold." We need to remember this, along with the words of Paul to his community that it is the Spirit that teaches us to pray, and prays within us always.

The Rosary is a string, with beads that mark out five sets of ten, with another bead separate at the beginning of each decade and at the end of each decade. The separate one at the beginning is traditionally for an Our Father and the one at the end is for the Doxology, or the short praise of the Trinity: "Glory be to the Father and to the Son and to the Holy Spirit, as it was in the beginning, is now and ever shall be, world without end. Amen." The ten beads in between are for reciting the Hail Mary. But the string can have any kinds of markers: beads, knots, seeds, flowers. At one time the beads were made from crushed rose petals or other flowers, hence the name Rosary. They are basically provided as an aid in keeping track of prayers that are intended to become habitual, rote, or repetitious as they are prayed. These can be prayed silently, aloud, softly, chanted, whispered, sung, even almost mindlessly. They are fashioned in a circle and so symbolize a continuous enclosure or continuity of life—the prayer and the life are dedicated to the one you pray to and are encompassed by the one who hears the prayers. Practically every religion in every part of the world uses these prayer beads, chains, rosaries, chaplets, or strings with knots to mark off prayer and to bind the one who prays to God.

Originally the Rosary was a prayer devised to help connect people who could not read and so could not participate in the Divine Office, or the *Lecto Divino*, of the Church. From the fourth century onward, monasteries held prayers seven times daily, using the one hundred fifty psalms of the Bible, readings from the Scriptures, prayers of petition for the universal Church, closing with the Doxology and the Our Father. Those who could not read wished to participate in this prayer. And in the beginning people would pray the Our Father one hundred fifty times over the course of a week, seven times a day, or whenever they could before sleep and after rising. Much more recently, it is said that Pope Paul VI once lifted up his rosary during a talk at the Vatican and said, "This is the Bible for those who can neither read nor write." The emphasis has always been on the Scriptures, drawing attention back to the Word of God, the Rosary serving as an interim, or bridge, to the Gospel for those who cannot read or study the wisdom of the Word of God.

Others began using the greeting to Mary by the Angel

Gabriel—"Hail, full of grace, the Lord is with you" (Luke 1:26)—combined with other short memorized prayers, pieces of the psalms, and short lines from the Scriptures about the life of Jesus. This devotion, in various forms and somewhat like the traditional form we are used to now, developed between the eleventh and late-fifteenth centuries. Traditionally one form is attributed to Saint. Dominic (1170–1221), who was very devoted to Our Lady. At some time, the second half of the salutation, the blessing of Mary by Elizabeth, was added (Luke 1:42) and eventually the word *Jesus* was inserted at the end of the salutation.

Around 1569, Pope Pius V recommended the prayer of the one hundred fifty angelic salutations along with the Our Father while meditating on the mysteries of the life and death of Christ. This pope is thought to be the one who added the second half of the prayer as we know it today, the words: "Holy Mary, Mother of God, pray for us sinners, now and at the hour of our death. Amen." The prayer was called the Hail Mary, or more commonly at that time, the Ave Maria. This form of address formally shifted the prayer away from God the Father, or Jesus, to Mary. In 1573 this pope established the feast of the Holy Rosary—sadly to thank God for victory over the Turks at Lepanto.

In the Eastern Church the beads are traditionally bound to the Jesus Prayer, which is repeated over and over, day and night. It is short and directed to Jesus: "Jesus Christ, Son of the Living God, have mercy on me,

a sinner." Or it is framed in the plural: "Jesus Christ,
Son of the Living God, have mercy on us, sinners." It is
physical, our hands fingering each knot or bead. It is ver-
bal. It is mindful. It is sensate. It seeks to bind together
body and soul, mind and heart. At one time it frees the
mind from distraction, returning it to the focus of the
prayer—reflection on the mysteries of Christ's birth, life,
teaching, death, and rising in glory. And at other times it
reminds us of how we drift from awareness of the presence of God, who is everywhere in our life and world.
Rarely is the concentration focused on the actual prayer,
which is said, mantralike, repetitiously, over and over
again. It is more like listening to a piece of music: you
rarely concentrate on the individual notes but on the
overall effect, which takes you elsewhere, to a place of devotion, peace, intensity, intimacy, and communion.
Touching the beads is like touching base, touching the
strings of a musical instrument that draws forth a depth
of sound that can, in turn, sound our own depths.

With concentration on the Word of God in the
Scriptures, the selection chosen for reflection and contemplation is read prior to the actual recitation of the repeated prayer: the Hail Mary, the Our Father, or the
Jesus Prayer. And there are some moments for silent integration, letting the Word seep into our minds and
hearts. After the ten prayers and the Doxology, there is
time for stillness again before the next portion of
Scripture is read and the prayer begins again. The Rosary
is circular and so it is not so much a task to finish, or an

end to arrive at, saying "I said my Rosary today," or "I said three, etc." but it serves as a guide along the way and it never really ends. It is intended to bring us back again and again to the presence of God and our being in God's presence always.

THE HAIL MARY

The prayer of "Ave Maria," or the Hail Mary, developed over thousands of years with the original focus on the angelic salutation to Mary. Contemporary scripture exegesis has discovered connections of the words with the prophet Zephaniah's announcement of the new kingdom of God that will usher in a time of justice and a reign of peace for all.

> Cry out with joy, O daughter of Zion; Rejoice, O people of Israel! Sing joyfully with all your heart, daughter of Jerusalem! Yahweh has lifted your sentence and has driven your enemies away. Yahweh, the King of Israel is with you; do not fear any misfortune.
>
> On that day they will say to Jerusalem, Do not be afraid nor let your hands tremble, for Yahweh your God is within you, Yahweh, saving warrior. He will jump for joy on seeing you, for he has revived his love. For you he will cry out with joy, as you do in the days of the Feast.

I will drive away the evil I warned you about, and you will no longer be shamed. On that day I will face your oppressors: I will save the lame sheep and bring the lost back into the fold. I will give them renown and honor in all the lands where humiliation was your lot.

On that day I will be good to you and gather you to make you famous and honourable among all the peoples of the earth, when I bring back the captives before your eyes—this is Yahweh's word. (Zephaniah 3:14–20)

These words of joyous hope and promise follow the description of a people that will await the coming of the One who will redeem and save them. The prophet says, "I will leave within you a poor and meek people who seek refuge in God. The remnant of Israel will not act unjustly nor will they speak falsely, nor will deceitful words be found in their mouths. They will eat and rest with none to threaten them." This is the remnant of the gospel of Luke who wait with longing, with all their hearts and souls and minds and resources for the promise to come true: Zechariah, Elizabeth, Mary, Joseph, the shepherds, Anna, and Simeon, among those named in the opening chapters. The angelic salutation to Mary is the announcement to all the remnant of faithful ones, in Israel and later in the Church, who wait for the Word to come true in the world, in flesh and blood. Mary stands as one of those who wait, a people who have remained hopeful and faithful to the Word of God. Our salvation, liberation, and freedom have always been rooted in the Word of God to his people.

And the prayer continues to develop and shift focus on to what is truly important in our belief. This is a rendition of the Hail Mary from South America, written down from the oral tradition by Jose Antonio Esquivel, SJ.

Ave Maria, of the third world, full of grace, all you who know pain, know the anxieties and the subhuman condition of your people, the Lord is with you, with all who suffer, who hunger and thirst for justice, who know neither letters nor figures.

Blessed are you among women, the women and men of the roads and pueblos, of furrowed faces, of brawny muscles, of calloused hands, of forlorn eyes, but with hope.

Blessed is the fruit of your womb, Jesus. Because without him, our life and the struggle for human dignity has no meaning.

Sancta Maria, all of you holy, a thousand times holy, by your lives, by the times you carry water, that you smudge your face at the hearth, trusting and hoping in God. He has made you Mother of God.

Pray for us sinners, for it is our fault, in one way or another, by our egoism and envy, that you, joined with the rest of the women and the men of

the poor, the third world, suffer misery, totali-
tarian governments, economic repression, wars
and blood and hatred.

Now, so that we change, so that there will be a
conversion of heart and of all men and women
towards your Son, our brother.

And at the hour of our death, so that the
Lord have mercy on all who have offended him in
our brothers and sisters, in the men and women
of a world which is struggling desperately for life.
Amen.

And the prayer must keep changing and shifting to reflect
the life of the Church, but even more, the life of the people of the world: a world where 80 percent of the people
are dying of starvation, and war is a constant factor of
daily life, and the earth itself is battered by destruction,
pollution, and wasteful use. In one of his sermons, in
speaking about Mary, Pope John Paul II prayed this piece
within a larger reflection on the Feast of the Immaculate
Conception, December 8, 2002, in Rome:

Sancta Maria, Mater Dei, ora pro nobis!
Pray, O Mother, for all of us.
Pray for humanity that suffers poverty and injustice,
violence and hatred, terror and war.
Help us to contemplate with the holy rosary
the mysteries of him who "is our peace,"
So that we will feel involved
in a specific effort of service to peace.

Look with special attention
upon the land in which you gave birth to Jesus,
a land that you loved together
and that is still so tried today.

Pray for us, Mother of Hope!
"Give us days of peace, watch over our way.
Let us see your Son
full of joy in heaven." Amen.

(Zenit, ZE02120805, Vatican News Service,
   on-line)

The prayer of the Rosary, no matter how it is prayed, must always lead us back to the Word of God and to obedience to the Father, since we are all baptized in the Spirit. The last words written of Mary in the Gospel of John is where we must always arrive when we pray. It is her last testament and words: the gospel gives her command. "His mother said to the servants: Do whatever He tells you to do!" (John 2:5) The intent of the Rosary is always obedience to the Word of God and a life that puts into practice the will of God that is the Good News of God to the poor of the earth. If we are truly the children of Mary then we must give birth to the Word of God in our lives and bodies, and like the Beloved Disciple, we must stand at the foot of the cross in our world, where we will always find her grieving over the sufferings and death of the children of the Father.

THREE

The Joyful Mysteries

"With an adorable, never-ceasing energy, God mixed Himself up with all the history of creation."

—John Henry Newman

These five mysteries introduce us to the Incarnation, the Word made flesh entering our world, our history, and our lives, reordering the human race and turning the universe back toward God and its fulfillment. John Paul II says in his Apostolic Letter that these mysteries are "marked by the joy radiating from the event of the Incarnation." (RVM, p.

27, #20) From this moment on, all of life, ordinary or seemingly startling, is the place of divine presence among us. Now God converges with us, interacts with us, accompanies us, mutually engages us, and is one of us!

THE FIRST JOYFUL MYSTERY:

The Announcement of the INCARNATION

SCRIPTURE

The angel Gabriel was sent from God to a town of Galilee called Nazareth, to a virgin betrothed to a man named Joseph, of the house of David, and the virgin's name was Mary. And coming to her, he said: "Hail, full of grace! The Lord is with you." But she was greatly troubled at what was said and pondered what sort of greeting this might be. Then the angel said to her, "Do not be afraid, Mary, for you have found favor with God. Behold, you will conceive in your womb and bear a son, and you shall name him Jesus. He will be great and will be called the Son of the Most High, and the Lord God will give him the throne of David, his father, and he will rule over the house of Jacob forever, and of his kingdom there will be no end."

But Mary said to the angel, "How can this be, since I have no relations with a man?" And the angel said to her in reply, "The Holy Spirit will come upon you, and the power of the Most High will overshadow you. Therefore the child to be born will be called the Son of God. And behold, Elizabeth, your relative, has also conceived a son in her old age, and this is the sixth month for her who was called barren; for nothing will be impossible for God."

Mary said, "Behold, I am the handmaid of the Lord. May it be done to me according to your word." Then the angel departed from her. (NAB, Luke 1:26–38)

This is the place where the fabric of history is punctured and the Angel Gabriel is sent to Nazareth, about ninety miles to the north of Jerusalem, to a specific woman, betrothed to a man of the house of David, Joseph. The messenger goes forth into the world with the announcement and a greeting, to a young girl, a virgin named Mary. In the older translations the greeting read: "Rejoice! O highly favored daughter." This is a daughter of the people, Israel, and she as one of them is invited to know the messianic joy that the people of the covenant have long awaited. This is the opening, the crack in time when the Holy One has chosen to enter humanity as a human being. John Paul II writes:

The whole of salvation history, in some sense the entire history of the world, has led up to this greeting. If it is the Father's plan to unite all things in Christ (cf. Ephesians 1:10), then the whole of the universe is in some way touched by the divine favor with which the Father looks upon Mary and makes her the Mother of his Son. The whole of humanity, in turn, is embraced by the fiat with which she readily agrees to the will of God. (RVM, #20)

This is the theology that has matured and developed in the many centuries after the moment, but the Scriptures describe a process and an experience that is to be universal for all believers, invited by God into relationship with the Father, the Son, and the Spirit. This is not just annunciation, but it is also conception, the incarnation of the Word made flesh. The familiar reading follows the ancient pattern of birth announcements in the Jewish tradition: the angel appears startling and disturbing. The response is fear and an allaying of that fear with words of God's blessing, and then the core of the message delivered in language filled with power and promise. Then there is reflection, questioning, even objections followed by an answer that is not necessarily an answer but adds to the message's portent in language of belief, and it ends with some sign of God's presence at work in the person's world that is pragmatic or helpful in taking the next step.

The pattern is found as far back as Genesis 16:7–12 (the announcement to Hagar in the desert wilderness of the birth and future of her son, Ishmael); and God's words to Abraham about the birth of his son Isaac (Genesis 17:1–20). In Judges 13:3–21, we hear the story of Samson's birth announcement. Farther in history among the prophets, we find in Isaiah 6:1–13 the confrontation with and call to Isaiah in the temple among the cherubim and seraphim and in Jeremiah 1:4–19 his summons to speak the Word of God to the people. The great, towering figures were announced into the world through angels' visitations to their mothers, heralding a new time in the history of Israel, God's chosen people. And the announcement and birth of John the Baptist, Jesus' cousin, is also brought by the Angel Gabriel to Zechariah in the temple. We often tend to concentrate on Mary's answer, but the core of the scripture is about who this person to be born is and what he will be and do for the people, and his relationship to God, which will change the people's and all the world's relation to God and one another.

When Mary is greeted by the angel she is taken aback, even deeply disturbed by his address to her, and ponders (a word that will often be repeated to describe Mary in terms of all that happens to her in relation to her child) what this greeting might mean. She is called "full of grace," a "highly favored daughter," and told that the Lord is with her. These phrases and descriptions echo that of King David, when the prophet Nathan tells him, "Go, do whatever you have in mind, for God is with you" (2 Samuel 7:1–5), when David decides he wants to build a temple for God. The prophets are filled with the Spirit, and those who brought the Word of God to Israel throughout the long waiting and expectations of the people knew the overshadowing of the Spirit rushing upon them, giving them a new heart to speak and lead the people.

Mary is betrothed, but not formally united in marriage with Joseph, of the house and line of David. She is a virgin and has not yet moved into Joseph's house. Initially she is confused, disoriented, and almost wondering aloud what this means for her, and for Joseph. She will conceive and give birth, and she will name the child, which was the custom in the Jewish community. But the focus and concentration of the announcement is on the one to be born: Jesus. The name means "savior of the people." And the language to describe the child is about a grown man with power, dignity, authority from God, a name and a person far greater than anyone ever born on earth. He is "great, the Son of the Most High. And God will give him the throne of David, his father. He will rule over the house of Jacob forever. His reign will have no end." This is staggering, awesome, frightening, and filled with the promise of all those who awaited the coming of justice and the presence of God, a messiah that would save them and once again raise them up as a people. He will be a king over kings, in the tradition of David, yet his lineage will rule forever. And most important, he will be called the Son of the Most High, son of God, in the tradition of the prophets, the sons of God that bore the word of God to the people. How can one respond to such power?

She questions, inquires, wonders, disturbed at being singled out. She is a Jew and knows her history and knows that God's word interrupts history, overturns lives, and reorders nations, and she will be deeply enmeshed in the will and work of God but does not understand how or why. She is from nowhere, an unknown village more than a week's walk from Jerusalem, the center of religious power and liturgy. She is nobody. Many of the medieval paintings of this moment have Mary with her hand up, shielding herself from the angel, keeping Gabriel at a distance, as though to ward off what is being said—it is simply too overwhelming, too much to take within.

But Gabriel continues and the answer of "How?" is pure theological language that has been used before to reveal the power and presence of God: "The Holy Spirit will come upon you, and the power of the Most High will overshadow you, so the holy offspring to be born will be called the Son of God." It is not an answer so much as a declaration of fact, and speaks of her child in relation to God, even more than to her. In the Exodus, the Most High accompanied his people as a cloud by day and fire by night, and whenever Moses went up the mountain to speak with God, it was overshadowed by a great cloud, mystery enveloping the one who was intimate with God. Mary is drawn into the tradition of prophets, leaders, and servants of God who obeyed his Word and surrendered their lives on behalf of their people. These words are as much a statement of belief in who this child Jesus would become, as proclaimed in Luke's community more than fifty years after Jesus' death and resurrection, as they are a restatement of the hopes of the Jewish people for the long-promised one who would be sent by God the Most High.

This is crucial for understanding Mary's answer: "Behold, I am the handmaid of the Lord. Let it be done to me according to your Word." She uses a word that we have misused and misunderstood, thinking of it in medieval and monarchical terms: *handmaid* or *maidservant*. But it is a theological acknowledgement, in awe and worship, of the greatness of God and submission to his will and word, opening to a future that is unknown and belonging to his design and hopes for humankind. Many of those who stood in faith before God used this word to describe themselves and their lives in the future after having encountered the Word of God spoken to them. The story of Moses speaking with God when he is sent to the people to liberate them from Egypt follows the pattern of this narrative (Exodus 4–14), and Moses is referred to as God's servant, or handmaid. In Numbers 12:7, Moses is described as "my servant, Moses, my trusted steward in all my household, to him I speak face-to-face, openly, and not in riddles, and he sees the presence of Yahweh." When Moses dies, he is once again described as "the servant of God, who died there according to the will of Yahweh." (Deuteronomy 34:5) David is often described with this same word, "my servant David," when God speaks to the prophet (2 Samuel 7:5), as is the prophet Isaiah (Isaiah 20:3). The apostle Paul will often refer to himself using this term: "I, Paul, a servant of Jesus Christ." (Romans 1:1; 2 Corinthians 4:5; Philippians 1:1, etc.)

This woman Mary stands like Moses in the presence of the Holy One, converses with God, and like the prophets before her, takes the Word of God within her, accepting the mission of bringing that Word into the world and living out her life in faithfulness to it. But as the prophets of old bore the Word in their mouths, she will bear the Word in her womb and give birth to the Word of God made flesh, Jesus. Bishop Robert Morneau writes: "Somehow she murmured a 'yes' and life pierced her heart and lodged in her womb." So many of the paintings and meditative reflections on this moment of the Incarnation do not convey the turbulence, the disruption of her life and Joseph's, the disturbance that pervaded her whole person, the upheaval that will ensue, the pain and fear that will be a part of her life, bound to this Word, her child but the Son of God, the Word made flesh. We want the moment to be quiet, stilling, passive, instead of human, unnerving, risky, life-threatening (she could be stoned to death if she was found to be pregnant before marriage). She had to change everything: her hopes for a relationship with Joseph, plans for her future, the image of herself and, more so, of God, and from the beginning she will ponder what any of this, what all of this means for her, those connected to her, and all her people.

Saint Ambrose wrote: "Christ has but one mother in

the flesh but we all bring forth Christ in faith." We ponder these words, their meaning, and their seeding of the Incarnation in our hearts and lives with Mary. This Word made flesh is conceived in our hearts and we are to carry this Word to fruition and birth into a world that suffers and waits for his presence now. With every word of the Scriptures that we hear, we are summoned, disturbed, and greeted with joy. And it is our time to submit, obey, and declare that we are the handmaids, the servants, of God, and our lives will be ruled by this Word made flesh, this Word, incarnated in us now. These remarkable mysteries are seeded and hidden in each of us, abiding their time to be brought forth, and it is not so much anything that we do, but what God is always doing in us, and with us, for the saving and gracing of the world.

We break forth into silent song with all those who believe in this God who comes to us, and declare for all to hear that we are the servants of this God, overshadowed by the Holy One, filled with the grace of the Spirit and bearing the Word of God into the world.

I will sing forever, O Lord, of your love
And proclaim your faithfulness from age to age.
I will declare how steadfast is your love,
How firm your faithfulness.
You said, "I have made a covenant with David, my chosen one;
I have made a pledge to my servant. I establish his descendants
  forever;
I build his throne for all generations. (Psalm 89:1–5)

Let us pray: "Jesus, Savior and Son of the Most High God, we ponder Gabriel's greeting that we are "full of grace and that You our God is with us" as Mary did on hearing the Good News of the Incarnation, of God the Father sending his beloved child into the world through the overshadowing of the Spirit. May we reflect upon this mystery of the Word seeded in each of us at our baptisms and gladly become your servants among your people today. May we rejoice with Mary and with all the earth that you have come to us in the person of your Beloved Son, in the Word made flesh among us, and in the Word of the Scriptures. May we take this Word into our own hearts and bear you into the world. Amen."

THE SECOND JOYFUL MYSTERY:

The Visitation of the Word

SCRIPTURE

Mary set out in haste into the hill country to a town in Judah, where she entered the house of Zechariah and greeted Elizabeth, her kinswoman. When Elizabeth heard Mary's greeting, the baby stirred within her womb. Elizabeth was filled with the Holy Spirit and cried out in a loud voice, "Blessed are you among women and blessed is the child of your womb. Who am I that the mother of

my Lord should come to me? The moment I
heard your voice, the baby within me stirred for
joy." Blessed is she who trusts God's words to her
will be fulfilled.
Luke 1:39–45

> *"Full of the Divine Word, the pregnant Virgin*
> *comes along the way, if you give her shelter."*

> —SAN JUAN DE LA CRUZ,
> DOCTOR DE LA IGLESIA,
> OBRAS COMPLETAS (MADRID,
> SPAIN: BIBLIOTECA DE AUTORES
> CRISTIANOS, 1991), P. 142

We are warned about the urgency and need to go to
Elizabeth and Zechariah's house with the opening words
that Mary "set out in haste for the hill country," for with
her acceptance of the Word of God into her person, to be
born of her body, both her life and the life of her child
are in mortal danger. The Word signals a change in all
plans, those of nations and governments, those of people
who have waited long, and now specifically in the lives of
these two women and their children yet to be born. And
immediately the impossible begins: both women, the
older Elizabeth, long-childless wife of the priest Zechariah, and Mary, the young unmarried and suddenly
pregnant woman, have welcomed with joy the coming
birth of their children, who are bound intimately to the
will of God for his children, Israel. And because each has

submitted to being a part of these wondrous ways of God, they and their children are intimately bound up together now and for the rest of their lives.

Elizabeth is rejoicing because the curse and long humiliation of her barrenness has been lifted, and this child has been summoned as a prophet from of old, from his mother's womb to "go before the face of the Lord and prepare his ways" in the tradition of Isaiah. Mary is rejoicing and pondering what this child conceived by the power of God will mean for her people and more immediately for her own life. She is pregnant with a child, but also with the Divine Word, the beloved Son of God in the Trinity and the One who always comes toward us. These women are blessed in their children, blessed in their faithfulness and obedience, blessed among their people, blessed as prophets of the Word of God, blessed as disciples of the Word, and blessed as those who are the first to know the presence of God loose in history in ways that not even the promises had suspected.

Mary would have slipped in with a caravan for the near-ninety-mile walk to the edges of Jerusalem, a difficult and hazardous journey for anyone, let alone a young woman about twelve years of age. It was probably a week's walk or longer. This is the introduction to Luke's gospel that is carefully crafted around journeys, the way to Jerusalem and the way of the cross and the way of Jesus to the Father. Mary, as believer and disciple of the Word made flesh, begins immediately on her journey of faith, bearing the hope of the nations and the promise growing beneath her heart. The first steps begin in response to the proclamation that "nothing will be impossible with God," and amazing, wild hopes immediately begin to come true in Mary's life and those of the people she meets along the way.

She arrives at Elizabeth's house and customarily greets her with the Jewish words of blessing and welcome: "Shalom! Peace be with you!" This is the Word of God in Mary's mouth, speaking in her voice. It is blessing, but it is also a command. And the first to react, to respond to that voice, that Word made flesh, is John, yet to be born, and he "leaps in his mother's womb": he dances for joy! That is the voice that he was born to go before, prepare for, and stir the hearts of people to joy for, in expectation of God's nearness to them. Then the Spirit that has been sent rushing forth in Mary's greeting settles into and fills Elizabeth, driving her to speak as a prophet, crying out loudly. It would have come out as a shout confirming Mary's own acknowledgment and obedience but more important, confirming that this child in her womb is the Word of God made human flesh: "Blessed are you and blessed is the child of your womb."

But Elizabeth doesn't know what to do with this recognition, this knowledge that has been seeded in her by the sound of the Word of God in this woman who believed. She cries out "Why me?" along with every prophet chosen by God to speak his Word boldly. She describes what has happened to her and her child, testifying that the Word of God causes bounding, leaping, unrestrained joy in all who hear it. As prophet, she blesses Mary, but the language of blessing is such that it is extended to all who, as followers and disciples, believe that the Word spoken to them will be fulfilled in their lives, bodies, and times. The presence of this unborn child is fraught with power and hope, and all that happens even before Jesus' birth proclaims that the promises of the past are coming true, beyond anyone's understanding of this Word of God made flesh in Mary, and in us who believe and obey this Word.

These two unlikely women, ordinary Jews, part of a remnant of those who staked their lives on the hopes of the promises of God coming true in their lifetimes, proclaim from the very beginning that this mystery of God becoming human and dwelling among us will be extraordinary and unusual, not according to the ways of history and human thought but according to the will of God, who seeks out the weak and the unknown and makes them strong and free. It is mystery within mystery, charged with delight, freedom, and wildly unbelievable reality!

These two women, the first to hear, believe, and obey the Word of God in their lives, must have fallen into each other's arms, embracing and dancing for sheer joy. Two prophetesses carrying two prophets, not knowing what will happen to any of them but knowing that God is moving into the world and nothing will ever be the same again. History has been ruptured, a crack has opened up in the world, and God in Jesus has slipped in and even now, still to be born, the Word and Spirit of God is loose in every person and voice that speaks and hears the Word of God made flesh.

Mary does not speak at all in this portion of scripture, except for the traditional greeting, and yet even those old words are fraught with power and awe. Saint Augustine wrote: "Make humanity your way and you shall arrive at God." And in this visitation of the Word made flesh in Mary to Elizabeth and John, the strange ways of God begin to unfold; from the moment of the Incarnation, our way home to God, the way of Jesus and the way of the cross, lies in one another and with one another. Thomas Aquinas said that "it is better to limp along that way than to stride along some other route!" Everywhere the divine presence now lies in wait for us, in every person we encounter, every place, every situation. All the way home to God now is filled with the presence of God hidden among us.

Mary's presence, filled with Jesus' Word and Spirit, makes an ordinary moment stupendous, monumental, powerful. Words ignite and spark responses that make Mary, Elizabeth, and John witnesses to what God is doing in the world for all people. New life is stirring everywhere Mary's shadow falls, and her voice is heard because she carries the Word of God within her. Elizabeth's blessing hints at what is to come later in Luke's story when another woman cries out to Jesus, "Blessed is the womb that bore you and the breasts at which you nursed," only to be surprised that Jesus did not accept her limited blessing: "Rather, blessed are those who hear the word of God and keep it!" (Luke 11:28) Mary is the first to hear and believe the Word, but all those who come after are equally blessed in this new family of God.

The visitation of the Word made flesh in Mary to Elizabeth and John asks us what the sound of the Word of God in our mouth does to others who just hear our voice and our greetings? Do our words and conversations stir the power of the Spirit in others and summon them forth in prophecy and confirmation of the truth and power of God at work in the world? Does our presence and our voice confirm others' belief and set loose delight and joy in all who are around us? Do we go forth in haste and leave the comfort of our homes knowing that this Word spoken to us changes everything and we must go forth to those who need the sound of the Word of God in our greetings of "Shalom, the Lord be with you"? And when we gather as believers, are we stirring the Spirit and sharing the power of the Word of God in the Church, carrying it within us, reflecting on it and pondering what God is doing through our lives now? The poet W. H. Auden once wrote, "Words are for those with promises to keep," and oh, do we have promises to keep and make come true in the world now!

Let us pray: "God, you have always kept your promises to us in ways we could never have expected. In Jesus, the Word of God made flesh, your promises became a person, a human being born of Mary and the Spirit of God. Now with your Word seeded in us, you expect and hope that your promises will continue to come true in our flesh, in our lives and presence in the world. Father, you have always kept your Word to us. With Mary, Elizabeth, and John, may we keep our word to you and be words of joy and blessing for all the earth. May we always go forth in haste, filled with the Divine Word carrying your presence along all the ways of the world. Amen."

Alternative-ending prayer: Mary's Magnificat, Luke 1:46–55.

 ## THE THIRD JOYFUL MYSTERY:

The Birth of the Word of God

SCRIPTURE

In those days Caesar Augustus published a decree ordering a census of the whole world. This first census took place while Quirinius was governor of Syria. All went to register, each in his own town. So Joseph, too, went from the town of Nazareth in Galilee to Judea, to the city of David which is called Bethlehem, for he was of the house and lineage of David, to register with Mary, his espoused wife, who was pregnant. It happened while they were there that the days of her pregnancy were completed. She gave birth to her firstborn son and wrapped him in swaddling clothes and laid him in a manger, because there was no room for them in the inn.

There were shepherds in the same area, living in the fields and keeping watch over their flock.

An angel of the Lord came suddenly upon them and the glory of the Holy One shone round them, and they were very much afraid. But the angel said to them: "You have nothing to fear! I bring you good news, of great joy to be shared by the whole people. For this day in David's city a savior has been born to you, who is Christ the Lord. Let this be a sign to you: you will find an infant wrapped in swaddling clothes in a manger.

And suddenly, there was with the angel a multitude of the heavenly host, praising God and saying: "Glory to God in high heaven and on earth peace to those on whom God's favor rests." (Luke 2:1–14)

> *Jesus came on cold straw,*
> *Jesus was warmed by the breath of an ox.*
> *"Who is this?" the world asked.*
> *"Who is this blue-cold child . . . ?*
> *Is this the Word of God, this blue-cold child?"*
> —FLANNERY O'CONNOR,
> *THE VIOLENT BEAR IT AWAY*

The prophet Isaiah cried out in jubilation about the birth of a child who would stun the world with his very presence and would be the promise of God among his people, shattering the darkness of history and human hearts. The birth of any child is filled with the unknown and mystery, wild expectations and unbounded hopes.

But this child! We hear it thundering in Handel's chorus of the *Messiah* and in softer tones of "What Child Is This?" and in the even more quiet hymn of "Silent Night," in words like "Son of God, love's pure light!" The names of this child have been cried out for hundreds of years.

> The people who walked in darkness have seen a great light; those who lived in a land of deep darkness, a light has shined. You have multiplied the nation, you have increased its joy . . .
>
> For a child has been born for us, a son given to us; authority rests upon his shoulders; and he is named Wonderful Counselor, Mighty God, Everlasting Father, Prince of Peace. (Isaiah 9:2b–3, 6)

These are the old names, treasured and whispered through the centuries of waiting. But this child has other names. In the angel's announcement to the shepherds, the child is called Savior, who is the Messiah and Lord and his very presence upon the earth is peace on all those upon whom his favor rests! And in the last readings of Christmas Day, we learn the name that is deepest and truest of this child: the Word.

> In the beginning was the Word, and the Word was with God, and the Word was God. He was in the beginning with God. All things came into being through him and without him not one thing came into being. What has come into being in

him was life, and the life was the light of all people. The light shines in the darkness, and the
darkness did not overcome it.

. . . and the Word became flesh and lived
among us, and we have seen his glory, the glory as
of a father's only son, full of grace and truth.
From his fullness we have all received, grace upon
grace. . . . No one has ever seen God. It is God
the only Son, who is close to the Father's heart,
who has made him known. (John 1: 1–5, 14,
16, 18)

God has spoken one word: *Jesus,* who is the fullness of
the wisdom of God made flesh among us. Paul will state
in Romans 16:25, "I proclaim Jesus Christ, the revelation of a mystery kept secret for endless ages." The
Church prays, "While earth was rapt in silence and night
only half through its course, your almighty Word, O
Lord, leapt down from his royal throne" (Antiphon for
the Magnificat, December 26. Forever, men and women
have prayed the words of the psalms: "It is your face, O
Lord, that I seek; hide not your face from me." (Psalm
26) Now we see the face of God in Jesus, who has pitched
his tent among us, dwells among us, a child born in occupied territory, to an oppressed people counted like
animals in a census of the world. The background description of how this child is born contrasts the arrogance
of the rulers of the world with the ways of God. A child,
a mere child, wrapped in ragged, poor cloths, laid in a

manger, a feeding trough for animals, in a temporary shelter from the elements. The face of God gazes up at us, wide-eyed and then sleepy, gurgling, unable to speak, yet saying: *love*. This particular child is God's peace, forgiveness, and joy exploding in flesh out into the whole universe. This sign, this child wrapped in swaddling clothes that are echoes of the cords of death, his shroud, cry out that he is human, one of us, and yet the angels and the stars of heaven cry out that he is Justice, the Holy One, the glory of God made flesh of our flesh.

There is the mixture of the stark reality of his birth: no room even in the place of travelers, which echoes another room, a guest room where Jesus will celebrate his final meal among his friends. His bed is a manger; he who is bread for the world, bread of peace and food for justice, is born far from home and surrounded not by family but by animals and shepherds, the lowly and shunned of society. God's secret has been told and written in human flesh, and both exaltation and tragedy shadow the nativity of the Word of God. The angels sing glory as God erupts into history and yet, it is the insignificant and meek (the word means "nonviolent and lowly") who are first to hear the Good News, and their joy is the greatest.

John Paul II writes in his Midnight Mass homily, 2002, about why this child is born and who he is for those who have eyes of faith and can see the "grace of God that has appeared, offering salvation to all" (Titus 2:11). He writes:

Jesus is born for a humanity searching for freedom and peace; he is born for everyone bur-
dened by sin, in need of salvation and yearning
for hope. On this night God answers the ceaseless
cry of the peoples: "Come, Lord, save us! His
eternal Word of love has taken on our mortal
flesh . . . The Word has entered into time:
Emmanuel, God-with-us, is born.

The child laid in a lowly manger: this is God's
sign. The centuries and millennia pass, but the
sign remains, and it remains valid for us too—the
men and women of the third millennium. It is
the sign of hope for the whole human family; a
sign of peace for those suffering from conflicts of
every kind; a sign of freedom for the poor and
oppressed; a sign of mercy for those caught up in
the vicious circle of sin; a sign of love and consolation for those who feel lonely and abandoned.
A small and fragile sign, a humble and quiet sign,
but one filled with the power of God who out of
love became human.

This child is born for us, in a time, a place, a people,
and a history. Eternity limits itself in humankind. Many
of the saints have said that this birth is always happening
now because of the birth of the Word in God's child entrusted to Mary and Joseph. Meister Eckehart, the
Dominican preacher and mystic, wrote in one of his
Christmas sermons, "But if it does not happen in me, if
this child is not born in me, what does it profit me? What

matters is that God should be born again in me." And paradoxically, this child is not born just for us, but this child is the light that is life for all people, for all times, but especially for those who have dwelled in darkness. Thomas Merton writes in one of his journals a short piece that appears on many Christmas cards:

> Into this world, this demented inn, in which there is absolutely no room for him at all, Christ has come uninvited. But because he cannot be at home in it, because he is out of place in it, and yet he must be in it, his place is with those others who do not belong, who are rejected by power, because they are regarded as weak, those who are discredited, who are denied the status of persons, tortured, exterminated. With those for whom there is no room, Christ is present in this world.

> FROM "THE TIME OF THE END IS
> THE TIME OF NO ROOM,"
> *RAIDS OF THE UNSPEAKABLE*, 1961
> (COPYRIGHT ©1965 BY THE ABBEY OF
> GETHSEMANI, INC., NEW DIRECTIONS
> PUBLISHING, NEW YORK)

Our God comes to us poor, homeless, a refugee on the roads of occupied countries, in a nation humiliated, deemed without dignity by an arrogant ruler, anonymously, with only a handful of shepherds and his poor parents, who look at him with awe and ponder who this child will grow up to be among his people. Steve DeMott, a Maryknoll missionary, wrote, "It is through the poor that we can experience Christmas as it was really meant to be." Christmas was one moment that turned the corner of all time, and now Christmas is wherever the Word is born, the Good News is proclaimed, and human beings are as tender with one another as our God is with us. God is born as a human child, in need and lack, who lives and dies with us, flesh and blood and bone, heart and mind, and yet mysteriously, joyously, humbly, is the Divine Word and Son of the Most High God, God's Spirit and Truth, God's holy presence among us always. This babe is born and yet this child is what Dante Alighieri writes of in his *Paradiso*: "I believe in one God—sole, eternal. He who, motionless, moves all the heavens with his love and desire. This is the origin, this is the spark that then extends into a vivid flame and, like a star in heaven, glows in me."

God's sanctuary, God's temple, God's dwelling place is within every human being now, and this Word made flesh invites us to worship him in spirit and in truth, giving birth to the Word in our own flesh and tendering the flesh of every other human being. This is the time now, for Mary to deliver her child, wrapping him in swaddling clothes, laying him in a manger, bringing God's Word of peace into history.

Let us pray. "With the birth of your Word, O Father, you sing a lullaby of peace and security to us, with words of light, of life and love wrapped in flesh of our flesh and blood of our blood and bone of our bone. Your son's first cry shattered the dark of night and with his first breath all your promises have come true. Now, with every word we speak, every breath we take, every song and prayer we make, every thing we do, may we obey your Word made flesh among us and give birth to your Word in us, in our history and our world. With Mary and Joseph, may we stand and then kneel in awe before the God who made us, now made lowly among us, and sing to all the earth: Peace, Peace, Peace to all and Good News to the poor, for now your favor comes to rest upon us all in the joy that sleeps beneath the flesh of your Beloved Son. Amen."

THE FOURTH JOYFUL MYSTERY:

The Presentation of Jesus to God

SCRIPTURE

When the time came for their purification according to the law of Moses, Mary and Joseph brought Jesus up to Jerusalem to present him to God, as it is written in the law of the Lord, "Every firstborn male shall be designated as holy to God." They came to offer a sacrifice according to what is stated in the law of God, "a pair of turtle doves or two young pigeons."

There lived in Jerusalem at the time a certain man named Simeon. He was just and pious, awaiting the consolation of Israel, and the Holy Spirit rested upon him. It was revealed to him by the Holy Spirit that he would not see death until he had seen God's Anointed One.

He came into the temple, inspired by the Spirit. When the parents brought in the child Jesus to do the customary ritual of the law, Simeon received him in his arms and blessed God. "Now Master, you can let your servant go in peace; you have fulfilled your word. My eyes have seen your salvation which you have prepared before all the nations: a light for revelation to the gentiles and for glory to your people Israel."

The child's father and mother were amazed at what was being said about him. Simeon blessed them and spoke to the child's mother, Mary. "This child is destined for the falling and the rising of many in Israel. He will be a sign that will be opposed so that the inner thoughts of many will be revealed—and a sword will pierce your own soul, too."

There was also a certain prophetess, Anna by name, daughter of Phanuel of the tribe of Asher. She had seen many days, having lived seven years with her husband after her marriage and then as a widow until she was eighty-four. She never left the temple but worshipped there with fasting and prayer night and day.

At that moment she came and began to praise

God and to speak about the child to all who were looking for the redemption of Jerusalem. When Mary and Joseph had completed everything required by the law of God, they returned to Galilee, to their own town of Nazareth. The child grew and became strong, filled with wisdom; and the favor of God was upon him. (Luke 2:22–40)

> *The Christian mysteries are an indivisible whole. If we become immersed in one, we are led to all the others. Thus the way from Bethlehem leads inevitably to Golgotha, from the crib to the cross. When the blessed virgin brought the child to the temple, Simeon prophesied that her soul would be pierced by a sword, that this child was set for the fall and the resurrection of many, for a sign that would be contradicted. His prophecy announced the passion, the fight between light and darkness that already showed itself before the crib.*

> —EDITH STEIN

The life of Mary and Joseph continues after the birth of the child Jesus, and since they are first and foremost Jews, it continues with obedience to the law that guides and orders every facet of their existence with reverence and with responsibility: to God, to their neighbors, and to their community of believers. Mary and Joseph live their lives in faithfulness and so they begin

Jesus' own public life with the ritual of consecrating him to God. This ritual is both a remembrance of Yahweh bringing all of the Israelites out of Egypt to freedom (Exodus 13:2–12) and an exhortation that, in light of that freedom, all the children of Israel are to keep "Yahweh's law [may be] ever on your lips." And just as God spared the firstborn of the house of Israel in the plagues that besieged Egypt, so the firstborn now belongs to God. In a certain sense, this is the public acknowledgment of the child belonging to the people of Israel and to God.

This first visit of the holy family outside the confines of where they have been staying is to the temple in Jerusalem, the house of God. Every family, every first-born child, is "handed over" to God in thankfulness for the memory of freedom and in expectation of the coming of freedom that will be ever more abundant. The offering that Mary and Joseph give is that of the poor, who cannot afford to give a lamb (Leviticus 12:1–8). But what is remarkable in Luke's account is that no one in authority recognizes this child, no priest or Levite. Those who recognize him as the promise are those who have waited in hope, like the shepherds, ordinary people whose lives are rooted in obedience, enduring grace, and the steadfast hope that the Word of God, given to the people through the prophets, will one day be reality.

This is Luke's version of the Epiphany account, the revelation of who this child really is, and a glimpse of who will come to know him and believe in him. It begins with the old holy man Simeon and the holy widow Anna. *Epiphany* means "manifestation," or "showing forth." It is a phrase that in religious terms means to be illumined or enlightened by the Spirit of God or the glory of God. It is God showing human beings what is the inner truth of reality, letting the light shine forth so that it is perceived in such a way that it casts insight into not only the present but the future, for all of history. The glory of God concealed in this child illumines Simeon and Anna, who in turn praise God in thankfulness and turn to share that insight and knowledge with all those around them. And in the case of Simeon, the light that settles in his old soul turns after his prayer toward Mary, who still has much to live and learn from this child she has brought forth in obedience.

He tells her, in language that echoes the Angel Gabriel's at the Annunciation of the Incarnation, more detail about who this child is and how Israel and all the world will react to his presence. And his account is filled with both light and ominous shadows and the looming threat of rejection, truth-telling and the consequences that will attend on that: the fall and rise of many in Israel. This light will penetrate the darkness, the coldness and the violence of the world, and all will be revealed truthfully for who they are and what they do, in the eyes of God. The child's presence itself is Light before the child ever utters a word. Association, closeness to this child will incur consequences that will radically alter the lives of those who love him.

Simeon's prophecy is hard, blending the ordinary—
the birth of this child—with the extraordinary—the power
this child will yield with his Word and presence. And this
child will save and bring peace to every corner of the earth
and truth to every nation. But this child will also disrupt,
contradict the powers of the world, and cause division,
dissension, and unrest, demanding decisions and commitment: a choice for the Light or a choice for the shadows and lies of the world. And specifically "this child" will
impact Mary, his mother, and anyone who brings this
Word into the world, aligning themselves closely with this
truth as essential to their lives and beings. This is intimation of the cross, when Jesus will stand hung on wood,
and Mary and those who love Jesus will stand with the
sword of grief and agony beside him. This will be a defin-
ing moment when all men and women will have to decide
if they stand in the light or against it.

But it is not just that one moment, this experience of
having to choose, having to commit oneself to the light
that is God's revelation to the nations. It will be every
moment of everyone's life. This child consecrated, according to the law, is the Word of God made flesh, and
that Word, which has often been described as a "double-
edged sword" of truth, will lay bare the hearts and souls of
everyone. This child is dangerous, the sword of truth
wielded by the arm of God, concealed in human flesh but
nonetheless revealing the judgment, salvation, and nonviolent power of God. This Word of God, in this child
and in scripture, will both reveal the secret thoughts of

many and conceal ever-deeper meanings of truth, of love, and peace. This child lives not only for Israel, but his people are all peoples for all times, and his coming and his presence will upset and redesign history for those who believe.

Simeon and Anna are the stars that point out definitively who this child is for Mary and Joseph. They allow these old, wondering, and deliriously happy people who now have experienced liberation and freedom hold him in their arms as they burst into song and praise God. They are "radiant at what they see." (Isaiah 60:5a) The gift of the Incarnation belongs to all. This child is "born of a woman, born under the law" (Galatians 4:7) but is also the beloved child of God, the Son of the Most High. Their eyes have seen God incarnate and they know it! The Spirit has given them the sight of belief and knowledge, and they begin to share that with all who are there.

Joseph and Mary are just ordinary believers, obeying the precepts of the law, and in the community of believers they are given revelation, as surely as they were given so singularly knowledge of the child in their dreams and the words of the Angel Gabriel before the child was born. Revelation's usual place is in the community, in worship and in the Word of God made flesh among us, and is found in every situation and aspect of our lives. This child "is the consolation of Israel," the servant of liberation and freedom and the glory of God made manifest. Simeon's eyes see not just a newborn child wrapped in swaddling clothes, the child of a poor couple, just weeks old; he sees the Good News of God and boldly proclaims the gospel for all to hear and see with him. The time of liberation has come. His words, especially his words to Mary, echo her own words of prayer when she stood in the presence of Elizabeth and John: this child will act with power and "tear down the mighty from their thrones and raise up the lowly; fill the hungry with good things and send the rich away empty; and scatter the proud of heart in their conceit." (Luke 1:51–53)

And the woman Anna, who is eighty-four (the number twelve, the tribes of Israel multiplied by seven, the number that constitutes infinity, completeness), who has fasted, living on hope and the words of Yahweh, comes forward and prays in the priestly tradition, acknowledging this child on behalf of all the community, which has struggled in the midst of so much despair and oppression for deliverance. As the story began with one young woman praising God for what he had done and would still do for the people, it comes to a close with an old woman praising God for deliverance and describing what this child will do. Their inner convictions and loyalties have been vindicated. God has come to them intimately and strongly. This is epiphany and pentecost on a small scale and it hints at what will come in fullness at the end of this child's life: death, and resurrection. But you must have the eyes of faith to see.

Let us pray. "O God, you made Simeon and Anna radiant torches, candle flames clothed in long robes of hope and endurance who cast light into a weary and tired

world. Their faithfulness was sparked by your very presence to erupt into words of gratitude, and awe at your
glory and goodness to us all. Your Spirit came upon them
when they laid eyes of faith on the child that Mary and
Joseph held in their arms. They took the child, the Word
made flesh, into their own arms and lifted him high in
acknowledgment of your glory dwelling among us. And
after long years of struggle they knew that more demands
and choices lay ahead for anyone who would take this
child, your Word made flesh, into their hearts. And they
spoke truthfully of the sword that would lay bare the heart
of Mary and all those who would stand in the presence of
this child, grown to be a human being. Let us learn to see
your epiphany, your glory, and your Word in all the people and places of our lives, and to give constant praise to
your goodness so that others may come to know you, who
are peace dwelling among us now and until forever.
Amen."

THE FIFTH JOYFUL MYSTERY:

*The Finding of the Young Man Jesus in the Temple
in Jerusalem*

SCRIPTURE

Every year the parents of Jesus went to Jerusalem
for the Feast of the Passover, as was customary.

And when Jesus was twelve years old, he went up with them according to the custom for this feast. After the festival was over, they returned, but the boy Jesus remained in Jerusalem and his parents did not know it.

They thought he was in the company and after walking the whole day they looked for him among their relatives and friends. As they did not find him, they went back to Jerusalem searching for him, and on the third day they found him in the Temple, sitting among the teachers, listening to them, and asking questions. And all the people were amazed at his understanding and his answers.

His parents were very surprised when they saw him and his mother said to him, "Son, why have you done this to us? Your father and I were very worried while searching for you." Then he said to them, "Why were you looking for me? Do you not know that I must be in my Father's house?" But they did not understand this answer.

Jesus went down with them, returning to Nazareth, and he continued to be subject to them. As for his mother, she kept all these things in her heart. And Jesus increased in wisdom and age, and in divine and human favor. (Luke 2:41–52)

> "What do you plan to do with your one wild and precious life?"

> —MARY OLIVER, POET

This is the last of the joyful mysteries and yet, like the one that preceded it, it is fraught with images and intimations of the future, of the rest of the Gospels and what is to come. In his Apostolic Letter, John Paul II sums up these last two mysteries of joy with these words:

The final two mysteries, while preserving this climate of joy, already point to the drama yet to come. The Presentation in the Temple not only expresses the joy of the Child's consecration and the ecstasy of the aged Simeon; it also records the prophecy that Christ will be a "sign of contradiction" for Israel and that a sword will pierce his mother's heart (cf. Luke 2:34–35). Joy mixed with drama marks the fifth mystery, the finding of the twelve-year-old Jesus in the Temple. Here he appears in his divine wisdom as he listens and raises questions, already in effect one who "teaches." The revelation of his mystery as the Son wholly dedicated to his Father's affairs proclaims the radical nature of the Gospel, in which even the closest of human relationships are challenged by the absolute demands of the Kingdom. Mary and Joseph, fearful and anxious, "did not understand" his words. (Luke 2:50)

Mary and Joseph give their firstborn to God and return home to Nazareth and live among their neighbors. Years pass and the child grows. These are called the hidden years, but they really aren't hidden. They are formative and crucial for Jesus' development and maturation as a religious human being. They are lived in a village, Nazareth, in the synagogue services, in the streets and homes of his neighbors and friends of his family and his relatives. He lives in a backwater town, under the eye of the Roman soldiers, growing up as a poor child in occupied terrority, oppressed and knowing what it is like to be a part of a people downtrodden, taxed, and careful all the time. He is a Jew, so his life revolves around the festivals and Sabbaths, and especially around the central Feast of Passover every year, when the whole nation prays fervently for liberation and freedom and seeks solace in the Scriptures, waiting for the one who will set them free.

Jesus came among us as a human being and he was among us as child, and as a young man. Like so many in the countries of Africa, South America, and Southeast Asia, he was hungry and lived a precarious existence. He probably worked from long before he was twelve, struggling with his family to simply survive in a country occupied by a foreign army that was brutal and dismissive of his culture, his language, his heritage, his hopes, and his religion. Like so many in the West Bank of Palestine today (where he lived) and in Iraq and other Middle Eastern countries, he knew insecurity, terrorism, and the machinations of the powerful and wealthy and their designs on his life, his future, and his people. He lived, as do so many young people who comprise more than half the population of such countries as the Philippines, Nicaragua, and Iraq, among others, with an uncertain future. Timothy Radcliffe, a Dominican, preached once that "Youthfulness is said to be the characteristic of hope, because to hope is to be ready for a future which is always open and long, however old one may be." (Sermon on Christmas Day, 2002) This child growing to be an adult is hope in flesh and blood and bone.

Jesus lives, just lives, for twelve years and then goes to Jerusalem to be with his people as they celebrate Passover together. He has prayed the psalms and studied and taken to heart the laws, the Torah, and the Word of God passed on through the prophets and in the promises given to his people. He has done good works and sought to integrate the knowledge of his religion with its practice, and we have been told that he "grew in stature and strength and was filled with wisdom: the grace of God was upon him." (Luke 2:40) When the festival is over and others turn to go back to their lives, Jesus remains in the Temple. This is a paradox: Jesus is the temple of God and he remains in the Temple. Jesus is the teacher of the covenant, the law, and the words of the prophets, and they will be fulfilled in him. This is the Word of God made flesh and he debates the word of the Torah and it traditions with his elders. They are amazed—both the teachers and the people who listen to them discussing their beliefs. His answers and his understanding are far beyond his years and study. They are born of wisdom, of the Spirit of God.

His parents journey a whole day before they realize he is not in the company of relatives and friends. And they journey another day back to Jerusalem. They lost sight of him, lost track of him, when they went back to their usual lives after the liturgy of the Passover lamb and the telling of the story of Exodus, the giving of the law and the seeking of freedom as a people. They return in distress and when they find him in the Temple, holding his own with the teachers, scribes, and doctors of the law, they are stunned and dismayed. His mother's words are a rebuke, filled with hurt. She takes personally what he is doing: "Son, why have you done this to us? Your father and I were worried while searching for you." They have no conception, either of them, who he is and what he is becoming, though he lives with them and is subject to them, learning from them. They are unaware of his meaning, his truth, and his vocation: that he has been sent into the world by his Father to save and bring life ever more abundantly into the lives of everyone, especially those whose lives are rooted in seeking the face of God and doing the will of God. Jesus' answer reveals that he has come of age and knows himself and God in ways that cannot be learned in study of books, traditions, history, or even from others. He knows that the Temple is his Father's house, his Father's domain, and that he dwells there. But his parents don't understand.

In many of the paintings in Padua, Giotto has a scene of Jesus standing before his teachers, yet singularly alone, asking questions and digging deeply into the meaning of the law and prophets. Mary and Joseph are on the outside of the crowd. Mary is portrayed as reaching to take back her child, to herself, her family, her world of Nazareth, while Joseph stands and looks on, wondering and listening. Years earlier they had obeyed the ritual of consecration by handing their firstborn over to God in this temple, but now that the child has chosen the Temple as his home, his way of life, and his future, there is much for his parents to learn about who he truly is—their child, yet the child of the Father, of God and the brother to humankind. Mary and Joseph must learn to let go of their child for he is God's beloved first and foremost, and they have been entrusted with him only until he grows to adulthood and decides what he will do with his "one wild and precious life."

There is an icon at Mount Angel Abbey in St. Benedict, Oregon, called "The Finding of the Christ in the Temple." It is a portion of the temple, a corner, angled into two distinct pieces, divided by a blue column of marble. On the right side is Mary and Joseph and on the other side, the left side, is the young man Jesus. Jesus stands with a scroll rolled in his right hand and he looks to be taking a step toward Mary, who is questioning him— or he is firmly leaning into his answer to her. Joseph stands behind Mary, his staff in his right hand, and is bent in awe, as though he sees and hears something he has perhaps sensed but not known for sure before this moment.

This is the joyful mystery of the Lady's acquiescence, of bowing to her son's Word as once she bent before the words of Gabriel, and she will have to do it with every word he speaks and everything that happens in his life and so in her own life. And Joseph too yields in awe, glimpsing the revelation of his adopted child's true Father. They both must bend, and back away, allowing this child to grow to be a man and come into his own inheritance, gleaned from their lives and religion, but taught by the Spirit of God surging within him since his conception. It is the beginning of realizing that they must lose him, lose their ideas about him, their perceptions of him, their personal attachment to him, and truly, as all his disciples must, go seeking and searching for him where he is always to be found: in the presence of his Father, speaking the words of his Father and doing his Father's will and work on earth, bringing his Father's kingdom and mercy to all.

He returns with them, but this is a demarcation point, a benchmark in their relationship with him. He is no longer theirs: he belongs to God the Father alone and lives in that Spirit even as he continues to dwell with them and be subject to them. This is a mystery: that the Christ, the Word of God made flesh, is subject to human parents, a man and a woman who do not understand at all who it is that lives with them. And the response of Mary is core to the rest of the gospel: "As for his mother, she kept all of these things in her heart." (Luke 2:51b)

Three times in Luke's gospel this has been the way Mary, his mother who is growing into becoming his disciple, is described. First when the Angel Gabriel arrives to summon her commitment to giving birth to the Word of God made human, she is pictured as "deeply troubled" or "wondering what these things could mean" or, more literally, "pondering what these things could mean." (Luke 1:29) Then after the birth of the Word, when the shepherds come in from the fields telling the story of the angels' song and blessings of peace upon all who know the favor of God in this child, Mary is again described as "treasuring or cherishing all these messages and continually pondering over them." (Luke 2:19) And now, a third time, the last time we see Mary in Luke's gospel, she is left "to keep all these things in her heart." This is the attitude and position of a disciple: one who watches, who seeks understanding, who searches for meaning, who listens to the words of the teacher and to the Spirit within until understanding and insight are born.

The next time Mary is mentioned in Luke's writings is in the first chapter of Acts, when the Spirit comes upon the community waiting in prayer for the "power from on high to come," promised in the words of Jesus before he ascends to his Father. In between we are left with a vision of her spending her life, from the first moment the Word of God interrupted her until Pentecost, struggling to understand who this person she has given birth to actually is. She reflects upon the experiences surrounding his birth and his growing up, upon those who are affected by his presence and his words, trying to make meaning out of what is happening to her, and to everyone around him. Patrick Ryan once wrote in "The Word," an *America* column, "that [the] Virgin's willingness to mother a son in mystery made possible our adoption in mystery into the family of God." (December 19, 1992)

Luke makes Mary the bridge between the Jewish covenant of the law and the prophets, the promise of the Christ to come and the new covenant in Jesus' own body and blood and Word made flesh. She is a daughter of Israel and she gives birth to the new, but she becomes more than that: she becomes his disiciple, who is described by Elizabeth: "Blessed is she who trusted that the Lord's words to her would be fulfilled." (Luke 1:45) She must concentrate on learning how to hold on to his words, remembering them—putting them together with everything else that happens, together with the words of the prophets and the psalms—and to put her own life together with his words. She must come to the wisdom that his words are the Word of God and Jesus' flesh is the presence of God, human yet divine. She must increase in wisdom and age, and in divine and human favor herself, along with Joseph. This is the way of discipleship, the way of belief in her child, who is the child of God, who is brother to all the children of the earth. The heart of the gospel, the proclamation of Good News to the poor, now begins, and from here on, Mary is the image of all believers, of those who become the Church, who listen and obey, take to heart and seek to integrate all that Jesus taught, did, and was into their own persons, becoming beloved children of the Father, growing daily and continually in the Spirit of wisdom.

She now prays and reflects with us on Jesus' words and life, and we now pray and reflect with her on the Scriptures, the Word of God made flesh, dwelling among us, transforming us, converting us, and making us God's own beloved children. Mary is mother to Jesus, but she is also a daughter of God, as we are children of God. And together we seek to become disciples who pray to the Father in the power of the Spirit that makes us God's own family: "Father, may you see and love in us what you saw and loved in Jesus" (Preface 8th Sunday Ordinary Time). In the words of C. S. Lewis in his book *Perelandra*, "There is nothing now between us and Him." Now begins the long journey, the long and never-ending process of learning with "Mary who leads us to discover the secret of Christian joy, reminding us that Christianity is, first and foremost, *euangelion*, 'good news,' which has as its heart and its whole content the person of Jesus Christ, the Word made flesh, the one Savior of the world." (RVM, #20)

Let us pray: "Father of Jesus, your young son learned by grace and your own gift of the Spirit's wisdom that his home was with you and his work was your will. His words were born of the spirit of truth, and his questions sought intimacy and freedom, demanded ever-more-truthful responses of justice and holiness in obedience to the knowledge of the law and the prophets. His tradition and belief learned young put him on the road to a relationship with you that was so singular and intimate that every word from his mouth and every gesture revealed him as your own beloved son. Father, instill this gift of the Spirit of wisdom and strength in us, your other children, and may we, with Mary, become intimate disciples of your

Word in the Scriptures and in Jesus, your son, who saves
us and questions us again and again with the words: 'Did
you not know that I must be about my Father's work?'
Father, may your work be our work and, together with
Jesus, may we bring your work to completion with the
strength of your own Spirit. Amen."

FOUR

The Luminous Mysteries, or the Mysteries of Light

"We are living in a world that is absolutely transparent and God is shining through it all the time."

—THOMAS MERTON

THESE ARE the "new" mysteries of the Rosary, called the luminous mysteries, or the mysteries of light. In a way they could be called the epiphanies, or the mysteries of the revelations of Jesus Christ, who is the light of God, shattering the darkness of history, of sin and evil, of violence and lies forever. These are five of the many significant moments in the public life of Jesus, five incidents that are indicative of the mysteries of Jesus' teaching, presence, and work among us. These moments reveal whole segments of the gospel and are the substance of the four accounts of Jesus' life: Mark, Matthew, Luke, and John but which had been conspicuously absent from the traditional remembrances of Jesus' birth, death, and resurrection, in the prayer of the Rosary. John Paul II says that "each of these mysteries is a revelation of the Kingdom now present in the very person of Jesus." (RVM, #21) They are highlights, moments of intensity and power where the glory of God bursts forth to illumine and penetrate all of our belief in this person of God, Jesus the beloved son and child of God. These mysteries are pieces out of the Scriptures that must always be seen in their depth to begin to appreciate what they are saying and what believing in them can mean to those who "put on Christ" as the adopted children of God. These are mysteries about the Christ but they are also mysteries about our own lives, when "we live no longer for ourselves alone but hidden with Christ in God" when we are "buried with Christ in baptism" and rise again to new life in him.

THE FIRST MYSTERY OF LIGHT:

The Baptism of the Lord

SCRIPTURE

And it came to pass that Jesus arrived from Galilee and came to John at the Jordan to be baptized by him. But John tried to prevent him, and said, "How is it you come to me: I should be baptized by you!" But Jesus answered him, "Let it be like that for now that we may fulfill the right order." John agreed.

As soon as he was baptized, Jesus came up from the water. At once, the heavens opened and he saw the Spirit of God come down like a dove and rest upon him. At the same time a voice from heaven was heard. "This is my Son, the Beloved; he is my Chosen One." (Matthew 3:13–17)

Or,

At that time Jesus came from Nazareth, a town of Galilee, and was baptized by John in the Jordan. And the moment he came up out of the water, heaven opened before him and he saw the Spirit coming down on him like a dove. And these words were heard from heaven, "You are my Son, the Beloved, the One I have chosen." (Mark 1:9–11)

*"I am that living and fiery essence of the divine
substance . . . I shine in the water, I burn in the
sun and the moon and the stars!"*

—HILDEGARD OF BINGEN

This mystery marks the last Sunday of the season of
Advent, Christmas, and Epiphany and is the beginning
of what we call in the Church calendar "ordinary time."
It marks too the beginning of Jesus' entry into the public phase of his life and ministry and is in itself an announcement of who he is. This time there is no
angel—there is the voice and the Word of God that proclaims Jesus' person and what his relationship to God is
for all who come to believe in him. This mystery is packed
with elemental symbols: water, the heavens opening, a
dove, a voice from heaven, a conversation between two
towering figures, the greater bowing before the one who
is not worthy to even untie his sandals.

In the Eastern Church this is one of the primary
icons of Jesus, marking a beginning, not just of Jesus'
proclamation of the gospel, but a new creation, a new
heaven and earth, and a new making of human beings in
the image of God, his beloved son now flesh among us.
The words are meant to paint a vivid picture of what is
happening or to let us stand as though we were at a win-
dow opening onto an experience that we are privileged to
watch, but are drawn into deeply as well. There are the
waters of Genesis and the hovering of the dove and the

words of God that make creation out of chaos and then the first words of the first day. Listen to the original images: In the beginning, when God began to create the heavens and the earth, the earth had no form and was void; darkness was over the deep and the Spirit of God hovered over the waters. God said, "Let there be light," and there was light. (Genesis 1:1–3)

Jesus comes to the Jordan River, the waters, and is met by a prophet who describes himself in John's gospel as "one who is witness to the light, not the Light that is coming into the world." And later in Genesis (8:6–12) there is the story of the flood and Noah releasing a dove from the ark to see if the waters have receded, and finally the dove does return to him, but with an olive branch in its beak, and Noah knows that the earth is once again inhabitable and the waters have gone. And then the sky opens, the heavens part before the coming of the Spirit, and the voice echoes the lament of the people who have long waited for one who would save them and bring freshness and new life to the earth. "Oh, that you would rend the heavens and come down!" (Isaiah 63:19)

The words of God are echoes of those of the prophets and the psalms, describing the servant of Yahweh who is just and compassionate, and the king who leads his people to peace with justice. In the second psalm, which describes the struggle between the kingdom that comes from God to his people and all the other kingdoms of the earth, there is an oracle in which God himself proclaims his king, his power, and his choice for the one who will be lord over all the nations of the earth: I will proclaim the decree of the Lord. He said to me: "You are my son. This day I have begotten you. Ask of me and I will give you the nations for your inheritance, the ends of the earth for your possession. (Psalm 2:7–8)

Even more powerful connections are made in the Book of Isaiah, the book of the willing and suffering servant of Yahweh who will bring justice and mercy and be the presence of God with the people so clearly that when they obey his words, they will become a light to the nations. The description of this person is exactly who Jesus is and what is happening at Jesus' baptism.

Here is my servant whom I uphold, my chosen one in whom I delight. I have put my spirit upon him, and he will bring justice to the nations.

He does not shout or raise his voice, proclamations are not heard in the streets. A broken reed he will not crush, nor will he snuff out the light of the wavering wick. He will make justice appear in truth.

He will not waver or be broken until he has established justice on earth: the islands are waiting for his law. Thus says God, Yahweh, who created the heavens and stretched them out, who spread the earth and all that comes from it, who gives life and breath to those who walk on it; I, Yahweh, have called you for the victory of justice: I will hold your hand to make you firm; I will make you as a covenant to the people, and as a light to the nations, to open eyes that do not see, to free captives from prison, to bring out to light those who sit in darkness.

I am Yahweh, that is my name, I will not give my glory to another; or my praise to graven images. See, the former things have come to pass, and new things do I declare; before they spring forth I tell you of them. (Isaiah 42:1–9)

This is God the Father's witness and testimony to who Jesus truly is and the Spirit's presence in the hovering and moving air, as a dove moves the air as it stays poised in one place. This is the threshold of Jesus' entrance into his Father's work in public, speaking the Father's words and doing what he sees the Father doing, as though he were the Father's apprentice in the world. (John 5) And yet, Jesus is baptized as each of us is commanded to be baptized, to repent and be converted wholeheartedly to God's ways and kingdom. Jesus was born among us and becomes as radically one of us as possible, bending in humility before John. When he does this, the Father responds with praise, acknowledging that Jesus is beloved and that he is well pleased with him. The Father's work is now Jesus' work—it is the work of bringing justice to all creation, renewing its face and tenderly caring for all that wavers, is weak and on the verge of discouragement, despair, and brokenness. This is the work of repairing the world, restoring the Spirit to human beings, forgiving and healing, strengthening bodies and souls, and standing in the breach between all that is good and all that is evil, that is resisting wholeness and holiness.

And all the amazing stories of Jesus are our own stories! We are baptized into Christ, buried in the waters of life, and brought up to breathe in the Spirit's freshness and power to heal, to bring hope, to forgive and do justice. We too "have been seized by the hand of God for the victory of justice" and raised up to a life that is stronger than any suffering, death, or sin. Wondrously, we are given a new relationship with God in our baptisms, the same relationship that Jesus knew with his Father. We are now the "beloved children of God, with Jesus, born in the waters of the Spirit" and our Father says to each of us: "You are my beloved child, in whom I am well pleased!" In our baptisms we are summoned to follow Jesus ever more deeply into his light. Our baptisms are our initial immersion into the mystery of our being, created anew into a relationship of being the beloved of God, with Jesus as our brother. And so we are to practice what Barry Lopez says: "[make] your life a worthy expression of leaning into the light."

This moment of Jesus' baptism and the descent of the Spirit and the testimony of the Father are the lens we are to use to look at the whole of the gospel that follows. We are to keep in mind the words of the Father whenever we see Jesus doing something that startles us, confounds us, shakes us to the core, or when we are tempted to reject him or to take offense at what he does and says. This is Jesus' way: gentleness, meekness, nonviolent resistance to evil that harms no one, especially those most vulnerable, and yet, to bring justice. This is why he came into the world: to give sight to the blind, to stop prejudice, to wash out our eyes and make them see the suffering of others, make us sensitive to what is needed; to repair what is torn and to bring prisoners out of darkness and confinement. This is justice that is inseparable from its balance and counterpart: that is the fullness of God's power among us in the person of Jesus.

Jesus is the one we follow but he is not described as lord. Instead he is the servant that is most dedicated to those who are fragile and weak, and most careful of those who are faltering and falling. For this servant will one day stagger, yet not fall, under the weight of anger and hate, and who will one day endure suffering inflicted on him in rage, attempting to break his spirit and bend him to another will than his Father's. They will not be able to— he will be faithful and his Father will be pleased with him and his obedience, even unto death, death on a cross. (Philippians 2) Jesus' life is our covenant, our bond to God, our new breath and life force. Jesus now incarnates justice and peace on earth, and we are baptized into his body and called to be this justice and peace in the world, giving pleasure to our Father as once his beloved child did on earth.

Many years ago I found this short piece in a newsletter, and I kept it because it speaks so beautifully of a father's love for a child and our Father's love for all of us, mirrored in Jesus, and in every person.

The father and the child would come to church regularly and the father's practice was to hold the child. One Sunday morning in the midst of worship, the child was seized [and] writhed painfully . . . The father lifted him caringly, carried him . . . to the back of the sanctuary, where he stood still rocking the child tenderly, speaking to him gently until finally the seizure relented . . . There was no sign of embarrassment or frustration on the father's face, only love for the hurting child. And then [Bob Welsh, the pastor] said, "In that moment, while I was preaching, I was preached to. I heard God speak to my heart and say, 'That's the way I love you through your imperfections. I'm not embarrassed to have people know that you are my child.' " (Bob Olmstead)

God the Father is not embarrassed to have Jesus, his beloved, as his child, and God our Father is not embarrassed to have any of us as his children because of the Spirit shared with us in baptism. This mystery of Jesus' baptism questions us: Do we live in such a way that our God is pleased with us, and does our Father have good reason to look upon us and see in us what God saw and so loved in Jesus? The Spirit given to us in baptism stirs over us and calls us to bend before God and one another and walk with Jesus as his brothers and sisters.

Let us pray. "Father, you have so loved us, your children, that you have given your own beloved son as brother to us. And you have given us the sacrament of baptism as a mystery that initiates us into your own life, the life of the Trinity: Father, Son, and Spirit. You have filled us with your Spirit, who teaches us and gives us the right to call you Father. We stand before you, with Jesus, and pray with your own Spirit and seek to live our lives as your presence of justice and peace in the world, as once your Beloved Son was while he lived among us. May you look upon us as we bend our wills to obey you and seek to bring your kingdom. May you be well pleased with us who come before you today. And may we always live in the freedom of the children of God, as we publicly vow in our baptismal promises. We ask this, O God our Father, in the name of your Beloved Son, Jesus the Christ, and in his Spirit. Amen."

THE SECOND MYSTERY OF LIGHT:

The Wedding Feast at Cana

SCRIPTURE

Three days later there was a wedding in Cana of Galilee, and the mother of Jesus was there. Jesus and his disciples were also invited to the wedding. When the wine was finished, the mother of Jesus said to him, "They have no wine." Jesus said to her, "Woman, what do you want with me? My hour has not yet come." However his mother said to the servants, "Do whatever he tells you."

Nearby were six stone water jars for the ceremonial washing; each jar could hold twenty to thirty gallons. Jesus said to the servants: "Fill the jars with water." And they filled them to the brim. Then Jesus said, "Now draw some out and take it to the steward." So they did.

The steward tasted the water that had become wine, without knowing from where it had come; for only the servants who had drawn the water knew. So, he called the bridegroom to tell him, "Everyone serves the best wine first and when people have drunk enough, he serves that which is ordinary. Instead you have kept the best wine until the end."

This miraculous sign was the first, and Jesus performed it at Cana in Galilee. In this way he let his Glory appear and his disciples believed in him. After this, Jesus went down to Capernaum with his mother, his brothers and his disciples; and they stayed there for a few days. (John 2:1–12)

> *"Fill my cup, let it overflow, let it overflow with love."*

> —AFRICAN AMERICAN
> TRADITIONAL SONG

The mother of Jesus is present in only two chapters, two experiences found in John's gospel: that of Cana in

Calvary in chapter 2, and at the foot of the cross in chapter 19. She appears nowhere else. These two stories are like parentheses around the rest of the gospel, beginning with the first sign—the conversion of water into wine—until the last one of raising Lazarus from the dead. In all the other gospels, Jesus begins his ministry with the announcement of the coming of the kingdom of God and a call to repentance and belief. But John begins Jesus' ministry with this sign, sometimes called a parable, the story of a wedding feast where the wine has run out that speaks about time and its fulfillment and a celebration. The image of the wedding feast and Jesus' miracle of the wine are rich symbols of the covenant and the joy of the coming Messiah's presence and blessings of abundance and new life. It calls to mind an expressive passage in Isaiah.

> Yahweh, you are my God; I exalt you and praise your name, for you have done wonderful things, faithful and true, planned long ago. . . . For you have been a refuge to the poor, a haven to the needy in time of distress, a harbor in the storm, a shade from the heat. For the blast from the ruthless is like an icy storm, like heat in a dry place. You silence the noise of foreigners; you subdue the singing of the despot and the proud.
>
> On this mountain Yahweh Sabaoth will prepare for all peoples a feast of rich food and choice wines, meat full of marrow, fine wine strained.
>
> On this mountain he will destroy the pall cast over all the peoples, this very shroud spread over

all nations, and death will be no more. The Lord Yahweh will wipe away the tears from all cheeks and eyes; he will take away the humiliation of his people all over the world: for Yahweh has spoken.

On that day you will say: This is our God. We have waited for him to save us, let us be glad and rejoice in his salvation. (Isaiah 25:1, 4–9)

This is John's inauguration of the kingdom and the coming of the feast in the presence of the person Jesus.

And Jesus' mother is there. Nowhere in John's gospel is Mary ever referred to by name. She is either Jesus' mother or "the woman." It is she who realizes they are out of wine and makes that lack known to Jesus, rather bluntly. The dialogue that ensues between them can be interpreted in a number of ways. Jesus' response can be read as "What do you want with me?" or "How does this concern of theirs affect me?" These questions or statements are coupled with the phrase "My hour (or my time) has not yet come." In all the requests for intervention, for help, or for a miracle in John's gospel, Jesus initially is reluctant or puts an obstacle in the way of the one requesting it of him. It seems Mary is not an exception to this pattern. But he calls her "woman," which implies a relationship of tender regard and intimacy, closeness beyond or other than a blood tie. It is a title of respect and it is offered to those who are intimate with Jesus, so here it reveals that Jesus' mother is bound to him in a stronger relationship than as his mother—as his disciple and part of his community, which is coming to believe in him as more than a teacher, or rabbi, or, in her case, as her son.

The "hour" has always been seen as the "hour of the cross," the moment when Jesus is revealed as love and obedience in the face of suffering, rejection, torture, and even death. It is both the hour of pain and the hour of promise fulfilled. Mary is present at the beginning of this hour and when it is completed, on the cross. Mary doesn't so much ask for a miracle as make known to Jesus the lack and the need and the humiliation that will be heaped upon the bride and groom if it becomes public that they have run out of wine. She doesn't respond to Jesus' words directly but goes to the servants and speaks to them. These words are the last words of Mary in the Gospel of John: "Do whatever he tells you." They are echoes of the words of God the Father at the Transfiguration of Jesus, when the disciples overhear the voice saying: "This is my beloved Son, listen to him." (Matthew 17:1–5, Luke 9:35) The word for *listen* also means "to obey." This is John's transition or bridge between the old and new covenants, the old water and the new wine. Juan Alfaro, OSB, writes,

> More recently, however, the words of Mary have been looked upon in the light of the formulas for the ratification of the Covenant in the Old Testament. Cana is looked upon as a new Sinai in which the old water-law is substituted by the good wine. The people at Sinai had promised:

"Everything the Lord has said, we will do" (Exodus 19:8; cf. Exodus 24:3, 7; Joshua 24:16–28); Mary's words are an echo of such commitment by the people. (*Cuadernos Biblicos*-2, "Mary Woman—Mother of Christians in the Struggles for Liberation in the Gospel of John," Mexican American Cultural Center, San Antonio, Texas, 1979)

The parallels between this story and the one in Exodus on Mount Sinai are similar enough that both stories are meant to be read in light of the other. In Exodus 19:9, 11, we read that the people are told to be ready, for on the third day the Lord will come down Mount Sinai before the eyes of the people, and then Moses is told that God will come in a "dense cloud so that when the people hear me speaking with you they may always have faith in you also." And here in John, the wedding comes on the third day, and Jesus is invited to the celebration, with the story ending with the rationale: "thus did he reveal his glory and his disciples believed in him."

The story is intent on revealing not only who Jesus is but how empty and lacking our knowledge of him is and how much our worship lacks. The huge jars, used for ceremonial washings and rituals, are empty. They are then filled with water at the word of Jesus, and Jesus' word transforms twenty to thirty gallons in each of the six jars, more than 150 to 180 gallons, into rich pure wine—a surfeit, an extravagance, and a hint of the depth of Jesus' revelation in comparison to the watered-down version of what our worship and practice can be. The choice of words to repeatedly describe the servants is important. They are *diakonoi*—deacons. They are the ones who obey the word of Jesus. They are the only ones who know where the water comes from, and they are the ones who are aware of the glaring lack and what humiliation the situation can lead to, and that it is his mother that makes the perception of this need a turning point or a catalyst for revealing who Jesus is and what his presence on earth means for us.

The word *deacon* in John does not mean specifically the ritual function that it has come to signify today, but is used to describe people whose lives are dedicated to service in the community, and specifically those who follow Jesus' will and obey his words. Later he will say: "If anyone would serve me, let him follow me; where I am, there will my servant be. If anyone serves me, him the Father will honor." (John 12:26) It is the same word used to describe Martha, the sister of Lazarus, when Jesus comes to the dinner prepared for him in thanksgiving for what he has done for her brother: "Martha waited on them—or served them at table." (John 12:2) It is the servants who are core to this story. Only the servants *know* what is truly going on, and that it is Jesus who turns what could have been disastrous into a situation of rejoicing and celebration. The servants know the truth; as John will say, "If you live according to my teaching, you are truly my disciples; then you will know the truth, and the truth will set you free." (John 8:32)

And it is here at the wedding feast, the symbol of the

coming of the kingdom of God to earth, where justice, peace, and truth will reign, that the work Jesus was sent by the Father to do begins. It will be a radical change of what is taken for granted. The steward tells the groom that it's usual to use the good wine first, and then when the guests have had some and their senses are dulled, to bring out the inferior. But this is turning the usual on its head: now the choicest and finest wines have been held to serve at the moment of greatest need so that no one is humiliated; what comes last is far superior to anything that has gone before. This is John's revelation of Jesus, of Jesus' words and teaching and the will of the Father that Jesus obeys and teaches to his own servants. This is the Truth, and all that has gone before is lacking, especially the religious system that is "the usual" rather than that which transforms, radically alters, and sets in motion a whole new way of living that has unbelievable depth and breadth.

Jesus' kingdom has come with his presence among us. This is the first miracle! And all the signs, all the miracles, are promptings for conversion, to look at our lives and see what is lacking, what has become watered-down versions of the wine of our salvation, and through obedience to the Word of Jesus can become the best wine—what others need in their distress. We, the servants, are to be those who make sure that the banquet, the feast of justice, of peace, of mercy and forgiveness, of attentiveness to the fullness of life and love, is shared with everyone, especially those who need it the most, here and now. We be-

gin as witnesses to what Jesus intends to do—leave nothing as it was, fill up what is lacking, and do the work the
Father has sent him to do among us. We begin as servants
and as we walk with Jesus toward the fullness of his
"hour," we will be invited to a feast beyond imagining.
We will be called his friends—the friends of God who do
whatever he has commanded us to do. (John 15:15ff)
These words of Jesus to his disciples follow upon his description of the vine and the branches.

> I am the true vine and my Father is the vine-
> grower. If any of my branches doesn't bear fruit,
> he breaks it off; and he prunes every branch that
> does bear fruit, that it may bear even more fruit.
>
> You are already made clean by the word I have
> spoken to you. Live in me as I live in you. The
> branch cannot bear fruit by itself but has to re-
> main part of the vine; so neither can you if you
> don't remain in me.
>
> I am the vine and you are the branches. As
> long as you remain in me and I in you, you bear
> much fruit; but apart from me you can do noth-
> ing. . . . If you remain in me and my words in
> you, you may ask whatever you want and it will be
> given to you. My Father is glorified when you bear
> much fruit: it is then that you become my disci-
> ples. (John 15:1–5, 7–8)

These images of the wedding feast, of wine, of vine
and branches bearing much fruit, are John's way of

speaking about how to live in the kingdom, believe in Jesus, be related to Jesus and the Father and the Spirit, and to be disciples and servants, who are then called the friends of Jesus. This is the beginning of the miracle that is a drastically new relationship with God. We are to become the wine! We are to be transformed into the justice, mercy, peace, and forgiveness of God by obeying Jesus' words and imitating his way of living. We are to become as intimate with Jesus as Jesus is with the Father in the power of the Spirit. The wedding feast is where the transformation is set in motion, and its beginning will be finished, be completed, when Jesus hands his spirit over to the Father and dies on the cross.

The changing of the water into wine is not simply a miracle, it is a way of speaking about how to be the wine of hope, salvation, and freedom for all. Wine was used for medicinal purposes, to purify wounds, settle stomachs, and for drinking because water had to be purified. It brought people together and was used to celebrate turning points and moments of life both painful and exhilarating. It is Jesus' mother who points out what is lacking, what is needed, and what can be a source of humiliation and disaster. It is a moment of truth-telling in a situation where most people would have wanted to ignore hard reality, what was about to become an acute problem for everyone. What are we to do when resources run out, when people are experiencing great lack while others are unaware or insensitive to what is happening? So many people's lives are diminished by the experience of being without basic necessities—food, clean water, shelter, hope, dignity, a future that holds out life for them and their children, a life without humiliation, violence, and marginalization. Are we aware of the need all around us, while we celebrate, worship, and live our lives? Are we concerned like the mother of Jesus is concerned? Are we obedient to the Word of Jesus that calls for conversion, obedience, transformation, and hard work so that others may know the goodness of God the Father? Do we know the truth that Jesus teaches because we are servants in his company, or are we just guests at the wedding party?

This miracle, this sign, is the beginning. All the ordinary, daily occurrences of life are the places for transformation. The issues of nourishment, water, quality of life (being able to breathe, drink the water, eat the food), basic survival, as well as all the social systems of religion, society, and culture, are to be changed so that there is rejoicing for all, especially those excluded before, or on the brink of being imperiled. And no one is to be allowed to know humiliation because of what they lack. People are not to be left without what they need, even wine at a wedding. This is the work of Jesus, the work of the kingdom, the work of the servants and believers in Jesus. And this is the only true worship of God. Like the mother of Jesus, we are to make the needs of others known to Jesus and then we are to obey the words of Jesus, the Scriptures first and foremost, and bear fruit born of our being bound to the vine, Jesus.

We are to become those who work the miracles, do the signs that lead to salvation and belief in Jesus. We are to be the ones who question reality, surface the needs, and do not let them take over the celebration that is life with one another and God. We are to bear much fruit and so glorify God with Jesus. We are to fill all that is empty—all those huge jars filled with gallons of water that became finest wine—with an inexhaustible supply of justice, hope, mercy, peace, forgiveness, and love that makes life ever more abundant for all.

The story ends with Jesus, his mother and brothers, and disciples leaving together and going down to Capernaum, moving on toward Jerusalem, and they are beginning to believe in him. The journey into belief, into obedience, in knowing Jesus, the glory of God among us, begins to be revealed as they head toward the cross. This is the last time we see the mother of Jesus, until she stands with others at the foot of the cross. There is the sense that she was one his servants, disciples, believers, invited to be his friend, and that that is the primary relationship Jesus wants from all of us. It is a relationship that is stronger than blood ties, stronger than familial ties, stronger than mother-son-daughter, husband and wife. This is new wine, a new thing springing up, an intimacy with God that is as close as vine and branches, a new way of worshiping and living in the depth of God's love.

Let us pray. "Jesus your hour has come to completeness for all of us you have invited into this relationship of love with you, the Father and the Spirit. We are privileged to live in the joy and intimacy of the wedding feast and to know where the wine of justice and peace, mercy and compassion, comes from—to know that it is sourced in you, your words and bread and wine and friends. May we learn the art of being aware of others' lacks and to speak the truth in all situations so others are not harmed. With your mother, who is disciple and friend to you and to us, may we make others' needs known in the community but then let us obey and do whatever is necessary, whatever you have commanded us to do so that others can share in and rejoice over the inexhaustible riches of your goodness and love for us. May we believe and live so that others come to believe that you are the glory of God dwelling among us. Amen."

 ## THE THIRD MYSTERY OF LIGHT:

Jesus' Preaching of the Kingdom and the Gospel Call to Conversion

SCRIPTURE

After John was arrested, Jesus went into Galilee and began preaching the Good News of God. He said, "The time has come; the kingdom of God is at hand. Change your ways and believe the Good News." (Mark 1:14–15)

Or,

Jesus acted with the power of the Spirit, and on his return to Galilee the news about him spread throughout all that territory. He began preaching in the synagogues of the Jews and everyone praised him. When Jesus came to Nazareth where he had been brought up, he entered the synagogue on the sabbath as he usually did. He stood up to read and they handed him the book of the prophet Isaiah.

Jesus then unrolled the scroll and found the place where it is written: "The Spirit of the Lord is upon me. He has anointed me to bring good news to the poor, to proclaim liberty to captives and new sight to the blind, to free the oppressed, and announce the Lord's year of mercy."

Jesus then rolled up the scroll, gave it to the attendant and sat down, while the eyes of all in the synagogue were fixed on him. Then he said to them, "Today these prophetic words come true even as you listen." (Luke 4:14–21)

Or,

At that time the disciples came to Jesus and asked him, "Who is the greatest in the kingdom of heaven?" Then Jesus called a little child, set the child in the midst of the disciples, and said, "I assure you that unless you change and become like little children, you cannot enter the kingdom of heaven. Whoever becomes lowly like this child is the greatest in the kingdom of heaven, and whoever receives such a child in my name receives me." (Matthew 18:1–5)

"The secret of my identity is hidden in the love and mercy of God."

—THOMAS MERTON

This mystery of light can be viewed as a movable feast. The three scripture passages chosen above are jumping-off places into the mystery of Jesus' preaching of the kingdom of heaven and the call to conversion that enables us to see the entrance and to step over the threshold into that kingdom that has been brought into the world by the very presence of Jesus. The entire four Gospels are the preaching of the kingdom, filled with parables, images, teachings, exhortations, miracles of healing, and instructions on prayer. John Paul II suggests the readings above and others that highlight the mercy and forgiveness of God, which is given graciously to those "who draw near to him [Jesus] in humble trust." (See Mark 2:3–13, the story of all the people surging around Simon Peter's mother-in-law's house begging for healing, or Luke 7:47–48, the forgiveness of sins of the woman in Simon the Leper's house who has washed Jesus' feet with her tears.) Other readings include "the inauguration of that ministry of mercy which he continues to exercise until the end of the world, particularly through the Sacrament of Reconciliation which he has entrusted to his Church" (cf. John 20:22–23, the words of the Risen Lord to his disciples in the locked room that gives them the power to forgive sins and bound those who do evil) [RVM, #21]. A choice of which portion of scripture to read or reflect upon for this mystery of light could be whatever the gospel reading is for the day in the liturgical calendar so that the prayer of the Rosary would be more closely connected to the prayer of the Church universal.

Many of the missionaries I work with tell me that it is the poor of the earth who offer us the possibility of experiencing firsthand the freshness and vibrancy of the gospel and of seeing the hope that it offers the world. J. Milburn Thompson reminds us in his book *Justice and Peace: A Christian Primer* (Orbis, New York), "Standing with the poor, being present to the poor, seeing the world from the perspective of the poor, working with the poor, this is essential to being a follower of Christ. Christians stand with the poor because God stands with the poor." So often we forget that Jesus' first priority when he is anointed by the power of the Spirit is to preach Good News to the poor. (Luke 4) The Good News is that God is human and dwells among us and that we are forgiven, but it is also just as surely food for the hungry; medicine, healing, and health care for those who are ill; release from prison and the chains of poverty, violence, despair, desperation, and the greed and avarice of others. Whenever Jesus teaches and the crowds surge toward him, he begins with the words of hope and freedom, of the love and mercy of our Father that we are welcome in the presence of God. But these words are often accompanied by Jesus' touching, healing, listening, bending down to care for the sick, the maimed, and the blind. He is notorious for welcoming the outcast, dining with public sinners, touching lepers, and breaking laws used to avoid reaching out to those in need. The preaching of the kingdom of justice and mercy, forgiveness and peace, was inseparable from telling the truth to those in power, and calling everyone from the greatest to the least to conversion of heart and life.

"Jesus appears preaching the Good News of God"—these words are startling when you realize that the phrase "Good News" originally was used by Caesar, who ruled so much of the territory in and around Galilee and Jerusalem. With Jesus' presence in the world, the order of all things is upset, and once you have heard the teachings of Jesus, you must make a choice: to either dwell in the kingdom of justice and peace for all, or to bow before the power of the world and worship a nation, a government, a way of life, an economic system, or live in fear of who controls your small area of life. The person of Jesus first and foremost demands that we choose who we obey and by whose authority we live. God's kingdom is now "close at hand." If we look at our hands, they are within inches of our bodies, and if we stretch out our hands, we have two choices. We can stretch them straight out in front of us, in a gesture that usually signifies taking something, or we can stretch them out to either side of us, or in any direction, until we touch another human being. That's how close the kingdom of God now is to us. In the mystery of the Incarnation—God become human as one of us, with us, we can touch the body of Christ in every human being.

The call to belong to Jesus' company of disciples is the call to repent, to turn from what we were doing and intending toward the will of the Father and the words of Jesus in the gospel. Always it is a call to turn toward those who cry out in need, in pain, in prayer and supplication. Toward the end of Jesus' public ministry in Matthew's gospel is the famous parable of the judgment of the nations, the parable of the sheep and the goats. Jesus, as the Son of Man come in glory, sits upon his throne of justice and mercy and separates out all the nations of the world into two groups: the sheep on his right and the goats on his left. They seem to be surprised at finding themselves in their groups, and even more surprised when they find out that they have been judged on what they have done to those who consitutute the majority of people in the world, those people we usually lump all together as "the poor." In Matthew's story they are described as the hungry, the thirsty, those in need of shelter and clothing; those who are sick and those in prison. What we have done for them or what we have refused to do is the foundation for Jesus' judgment of us, and whether we are given the kingdom of God to dwell in forever with the Father or are condemned forever to separation from God's goodness and glory. The story is disconcerting because the judgment stands whether or not we knew this was so critical to our well-being and our life everlasting. Jesus' words have rung like a summoning bell throughout these past two thousand years: "Whatever you do to the least of your brothers and sisters I take it you did it to me and whatever you failed to do to the least of your brothers and sisters, I take it you did not do it for me." (Matthew 25)

These people and what their presence demands of us is the Good News to the poor. The poor, the broken, and the suffering body of Christ are God's privileged presence among us, calling us to ever-deeper commitment and obedience to the gospel. As Paul VI said, "If you want peace, then work for justice." And John Paul II has added to this with these words: "If you want peace, go to the poor."

These works are also the basic foundational stones of doing justice. In *Pacem in Terris*, written more than forty years ago, John XXIII states that there are certain rights that every human being deserves just by the fact that they are human beings. There are seventeen rights in all but the first are the most familiar to us: food, clothing, shelter, water, health care and medicine, education, a job, human dignity, freedom to practice one's religion, hope for the future, a sense of security and well-being, freedom from violence, etc. Oftentimes we have referred to this work as corporal or spiritual works of mercy, basic practices of virtue that bring home to us that we are children of God in a family that takes care of one another, both as a responsibility and a privilege. The Good News is first about justice: giving people what they need and require and making sure that they are treated with dignity and compassion as God has treated us. And further, the Good News is about being as compassionate and as merciful to others, even our enemies, as our Father has been to us.

The spiritual works of mercy are just as essential. Some of them include: comforting the afflicted, counseling the doubtful, instructing the ignorant, bearing all wrongs patiently, praying for your enemies and for the living and the dead, ransoming the captive, burying the dead. These are the initial practices, the building blocks of discipleship. They develop into a way of life, and in community they become an alternative way of living within any dominant culture that seeks to remind everyone in society that the poor are God's presence among us and that our God is human, dwells among us, and suffers with us so that we can learn to be like him in our dealings with one another.

We are called to practice forgiveness, reconciliation toward all, remembering that we pray only to be forgiven "as we have forgiven those who are in debt to us." The demands and possibilities of conversion to the gospel are limitless—we are called to love one another as God has loved us, even unto death. We are to live in the freedom of the children of God, calling God our Father in the grace of the Spirit as we stand with Jesus. We are to stand and resist with all our hearts, and souls, and minds, and resources what is evil and what harms others, yet we are to do no harm to another. And we are to live under no sign of power but the sign of the cross, which is forgiveness, mercy, reconciliation, no retaliation, meekness, and lowliness (meaning nonviolence), prayer for our enemies, bearing our share of the burden of preaching the gospel, offering our sufferings for the world, picking up our cross and helping others to carry their crosses, and to love, love even unto death, because our God has so loved us in Jesus. This is the gospel, the Good News of Jesus, and it is the kingdom of God that dwells among us even now, as all who are followers of the Crucified and Risen Lord, Jesus Christ, seek to become more holy, more true, and more like him.

More than anything else, the person and the presence of Jesus in his preaching of conversion and the kingdom are revealed in the concept and practice of Mercy. The Good News is that Jesus is the mercy of God among us, which has reunited us with God and draws us back to live in peace and good order with one another. What is mercy? Thomas Merton, the Trappist monk, wrote in his book *No Man Is an Island,* in his chapter "Mercy," some thoughts to reflect upon.

> The Christian concept of mercy is, therefore, the key to the transformation of the whole universe in which sin still seems to reign. For the Christian does not escape evil, nor is he dispensed from suffering, nor is he withdrawn from the influence and effects of suffering; nor is he himself impeccable. He too can unfortunately sin. He has not been completely delivered from evil. Yet his vocation is to deliver the whole world from evil and to transform it in God: by prayer,

> by penance, by charity, and above all by mercy.
> God has left sin in the world in order that there
> may be forgiveness: not only the secret forgive-
> ness by which He Himself cleanses our souls, but
> the manifest forgiveness by which we have mercy
> on one another and so give expression to the fact
> that He is living, by His mercy, in our own hearts.

Mercy is the wine and the blood of the Good News. It is essential to learning the mysteries of the kingdom of heaven that is among us and still in the process of be-coming ever-more present and influential in the world. Catherine of Siena, a mystic and theologian who also cared for the poor and those who suffered from the plague, was strong in her warnings to the Church, its leaders and teachers, to practice mercy, both the corpo-ral works of mercy and the mercy that was healing balm for the soul, the sinner, and those who were estranged and isolated from God and others. It was her tender touch and compassionate presence with the poor and the sick of the city of Rome that gave her the power to speak the truth to the Pope and the bishops about their own need for conversion to the gospel. One of her most fa-mous refrains is "For those who believe that Jesus Christ is Lord to the glory of God the Father in the power of the Spirit, then all the way home to heaven is heaven!" The kingdom is here when we bring it, uncover it, and draw others into it. The Good News comes true when we are true to our baptisms and are continually converted as believers and as a Church to the presence of God among us, especially in the poor, and the body of Christ universally.

The preaching of Jesus and the call to enter the kingdom of God reveals a God that is human, compassionate, just, and truthful. Everything that Jesus preaches reveals his relationship to the Father, that he has shared with us in our baptisms. Our God is not like other gods. G. K. Chesterton, in his masterful way, describes some of what our God is like in Jesus' words and life.

> That a good man may have his back to the wall is no more than we knew already; but that God could have his back to the wall is a boast for all insurgents forever. Christianity is the only religion on earth that has felt that omnipotence made God incomplete. Christianity alone has felt that God, to be wholly God, must have been a rebel as well as a king. Alone of all creeds, Christianity has added courage to the virtues of the Creator. For the only courage worth calling courage must necessarily mean that the soul passes a breaking point—and does not break. (From "Bread and Wine: Readings for Lent and Easter," The Bruderhof Foundation, on-line at http://www. bruderhof.com)

Our God revealed in Jesus reaches that breaking point—rejection, torture, death by crucifixion—and then God the Father raises him from the dead! The Good News introduces us to the wondrous understanding that life is stronger than death, that justice and truth are stronger than violence and lies, and that forgiveness and mercy are stronger than retaliation and hate. In the end, it is love, only love and always love, and that love is the person and the presence of Jesus born to us and living and dying with us and exhorting us to believe! To repent! To stake our lives on God's ways in the world! To have courage and not to fear anything, for our God is always with us, and there is no end to the depth of his love for us. That is Good News! Believe it!

Let us pray. "Jesus, you are the Word of the Father made flesh among us, and filled with the power of the Spirit. You are the truth, the way, the life, and our life-line to God, to home, and to one another. Even when we sin, when we reach the end of our rope, or it frays and breaks, you are there to grasp it, tie it in a knot, and draw us ever closer to you. Your Good News says that earth is home now and you are here among us. And you are a God that reveals your goodness everywhere, but also loves to hide among us in the poor, the destitute, and those who cry for justice and hope. May we repent, turn our lives around, and daily walk with you, ever-more closer to you, ever-more mindful of your goodness, and ever-more intent on obeying you and being your mercy and compassion—your Good News to others, who so need a word of courage, of forgiveness and mercy. And Jesus, teach us how to love, like you love us, like you love God. We ask this in your name through the power of your Spirit, to the glory of God our Father. Amen."

❁ THE FOURTH MYSTERY OF LIGHT:

The Transfiguration of Jesus

SCRIPTURE

About eight days after Jesus had said all this, he took Peter, James and John and went up the mountain to pray. And while he was praying the aspect of his face was changed and his clothing became dazzling white. Two men were talking with Jesus: Moses and Elijah. They had just appeared in heavenly glory and were telling him about his departure that had to take place in Jerusalem.

Peter and his companions had fallen asleep, but they awoke suddenly and saw Jesus' Glory and the two men standing with him. As Moses and Elijah were about to leave, Peter said to him, "Master, how good it is for us to be here for we can make three tents, one for you, one for Moses and one for Elijah." For Peter didn't know what to say. And no sooner had he spoken than a cloud appeared and covered them; and the disciples were afraid as they entered the cloud. Then these words came from the cloud. "This is my Son, my Chosen one, listen to him." And after the voice had spoken, Jesus was there alone.

The disciples kept this to themselves at the

time, telling no one of anything they had seen. (Luke 9:28–37)

Or,

Six days later, Jesus took with him Peter and James and his brother John and led them up a high mountain where they were alone. Jesus' appearance was changed before them; his face shone like the sun and his clothes became bright as light. Just then Moses and Elijah appeared to them, talking with Jesus.

Peter spoke and said to Jesus, "Master, it is good that we are here. If you so wish, I will make three tents; one for you, one for Moses, and one for Elijah.

Peter was still speaking when a bright cloud covered them in its shadow, and a voice from the cloud said: "This is my Son, my Beloved, my Chosen One. Listen to him."

On hearing the voice, the disciples fell to the ground, full of fear. But Jesus came, touched them, and said, "Stand up, do not be afraid." When they raised their eyes, they no longer saw anyone except Jesus. And as they came down the mountain, Jesus commanded them not to tell anyone what they had just seen, until the Son of Man be raised from the dead. (Matthew 17:1–9 or Mark 9:1–8)

"The soul always stands ajar, ready to welcome the ecstatic experience."

—EMILY DICKINSON

John Paul II calls this "the mystery of light par excellence," when the glory of God shines through the person, the body of Jesus, and the voice of the Father commands "the disciples to 'Listen to him' and to prepare to experience with him the agony of the passion, so as to come with him to the joy of the resurrection and a life transfigured by the Holy Spirit." (RVM, #21)

In the Eastern churches, whenever this reading is proclaimed, the day is called a feast of bright-sadness. It is an epiphany, a manifestation or showing forth of who Jesus is to those he is closest to: Peter, James, and John. These three disciples are privileged to spend time with him, when he goes to pray, when he is in a smaller group than the rest of the disciples. And they will be the ones who are taken with him farther into the garden the night that he is betrayed and arrested. This reading is a glimpse of glory, the glory of God shining through the person and the body of Jesus. This moment of vision and clarity is sorely needed because Jesus has just started to preach to his disciples about the coming events of his rejection, passion, death, and resurrection in Jerusalem, and they are already beginning to resist what he is saying and reject outright the very thought that this could happen to him. Especially Peter is publicly adamant that this can't be allowed to happen. But Jesus has turned his face toward Jerusalem, where all the prophets have been persecuted and killed. He seeks to invite his disciples to come along with him, and share in his mission and walk with him to the cross and glory. They want no part of it.

Jesus has begun to lay out the demands of discipleship

and what it means to follow in his footsteps and be aligned to him publicly. He has been very clear, even in preaching to the crowds that dog his footsteps.

> Then Jesus called the people and his disciples and said, "If you want to follow me, deny yourself, take up your cross and follow me. For if you choose to save your life you will lose it; and if you lose your life for my sake and for the sake of the Gospel, you will save it.
>
> "What good is it to gain the whole world but destroy yourself? There is nothing you can give to recover your life. I tell you: If anyone is ashamed of me and my words among this adulterous and sinful people, the Son of Man will also be ashamed of him when he comes in the Glory of his Father with the holy angels." (Mark 8:34–38)

This is what Jesus has begun to teach and the disciples are dismayed. Just moments before, Jesus had announced that he was going to Jerusalem and that he would be rejected by the elders and chief priests and the teachers of the law and that he would be killed, but rise again in three days. Peter, the spokeman, "took him aside and began to protest strongly." In the older translations, this is described as "remonstrated with him." This cannot happen. This is not what Peter and the disciples had in mind when they began to follow him and hope that he was the Messiah that they had longed for and expected to overthrow the Romans, raise Jerusalem back up again, and make Israel a nation to be reckoned with once again—of course, with them at his side as advisors and counselors. Jesus turns on Peter and the disciples and rebukes them sharply as he says: "Get behind me Satan! You are thinking not as God does, but as people do." (Mark 8:33b)

Peter, the rock, has become a stumbling block in Jesus' path and he is told to turn and get behind him because he is not preparing the way before him, but blocking his path to Jerusalem and what he was sent into the world to do. It must have stung Peter and the others to the core. But they have already started to question, to resist and to hang back from what Jesus is teaching. From here on out they are careful and cautious, and it shouldn't surprise us when they fall asleep in the garden and seem to ignore what is happening. They started long before that night. It shouldn't even come as such a shock that Peter vehemently betrays his Master in public three times, saying he doesn't even know him, and cursing him, because he started betraying him in this moment when he realizes that Jesus' way is very, very different from his own plans. It is truly a day that is aptly described as bright-sadness.

Jesus has been trying to tell them that they are not listening to him—they are listening to their own hearts, their own agendas, and to what others want him to be and to do for them and for the people. They don't want any part of Jesus' words or the Father's will. This is the reason for the trip apart, up the mountain to pray; just the three of them and their Master. Almost as soon as they arrive, Jesus' appearance, including even the clothes he's wearing, changes drastically. He is transfigured before them. His face shines with inward light and his garments glow, whiter than bleach could ever make them. The glory of God is shining through him. The word *transfiguration* can be broken down so that it reveals exactly what is happening to Jesus and what they are seeing. *Trans* is a Latin preposition meaning "across, a bridge, through, over" and *figure* is the human body. So when Jesus is transfigured before them, the glory of God comes through, crosses over through Jesus' body—in a sense, Jesus' body is a bridge—so that others can see straight through him to glimpse the glory of God that dwells and resides in him all the time.

When they see the glory, they also see Moses and Elijah, in conversation with Jesus, speaking about his passage, or his passover, to Jerusalem. These are the two towering figures of Judaism. Moses is not only the law-giver but the liberator of his people, bringing them out of bondage in Egypt to the land of promise and struggling to make them a people of the covenant with their God. And Elijah is the prophet par excellence, referred to as "the disturber of Israel," his very presence calling kings and the people to an examination of conscience in regard to how they are faithful to the covenant, care for the poor, do justice, and honor God. These two figures are turned toward Jesus as though they are bowing in his direction. Jesus is the bridge between this covenant of the past and the new covenant that he is going to open and share with all the people of the world, sealing it in his own blood. As the people passed over in the Red Sea to freedom, Jesus is facing his own passover from death to life that will bring all of us to freedom and resurrection.

But they don't see what's happening. Peter pipes up with "It's good to be here" and "Let us build tents for the three of you." He would like to stay, to dwell on the mountain and bask in the glory. The gospel says too that the disciples were terrified and Peter didn't really know what he was saying in some of the accounts, but even as he is speaking, he is interrupted—by the voice of God! A great cloud comes and settles over them and the voice comes from the cloud. This is the image in the Book of Exodus when the power and glory of the Lord accompanied the Israelite people on their march to freedom, as a pillar of fire by night and a cloud by day. And it is God the Father who declares what is essential for the disciples to hear: "This is my Beloved Son, my Chosen One. Listen to him!"

It is testimony presented. It is a declaration. It is a command, a demand. Listen to him. Don't listen to your own faltering heart. Don't listen to the fear inside you that you feed one another in your insecurities. Don't listen to the nationalistic cries of a Messiah to make Israel a nation again. Don't listen to the clamor of the people who want someone who will give them what they want. Don't listen to the leaders who are sharply divided over Jesus and in collusion with the occupying forces of those who oppress the people. Don't listen to those who reject Jesus' words because they don't serve their own plans. Don't listen to anyone else—just listen to my Beloved Son, my Chosen One. The Word of God is in the mouth, the words, the teachings of Jesus. But even more, Jesus *is* the Word of God, his very person and body. Listen to him, obey him, follow him, honor him, watch him, and imitate him—only.

Peter and the disciples do not want Jesus' way or the Father's will. They don't want the way of the cross, of death and resurrection. They want the way of power, of revenge, of lording it over their enemies, their places right beside Jesus in an earthly kingdom. They're not listening to Jesus' Good News of justice for the poor, of forgiveness for all, even of one's enemies, of reconciliation and the boundless mercy and compassion of God. They are not listening to his invitation to become the children of God, peacemakers, healers, and those who lift up the brokenhearted of the earth, bringing them hope and the presence of God in their struggles and sufferings. They are not listening to him tell them that they must resist sin and evil and injustice, but they must never use the tactics and ways of the world, which are violent and dismissive of human beings' rights and dignity.

And then there is quiet. Silence. Nothing else is there on the mountain except Jesus. They look up and Jesus touches them, telling them not to be afraid and to get up, stand up. These are the words of resurrection—Stand up for what you believe. Stand before God and one another secure in your faith. I stand with you, there is no need to be afraid. They get up, but they don't say anything to Jesus. They go back down the mountain and discuss among themselves what all this might mean; what being raised from the dead might mean; who the Son of Man might be. These are mysteries to be pondered, reflected upon, and spoken about with awe, among themselves. They have seen Jesus, glorified, transfigured before them. It is a memory now, etched in their minds and souls.

The Transfiguration—that moment when they saw through the body of Jesus to the glory of God present among us—where do we see that now, here in our lives? We are the body of Christ through our baptisms, Eucharist shared, the gift of the Spirit. Do we live our lives so that others can see straight through us, our bodies, our actions and works, our words, into the glory and the presence of God? Can people cross over through us and know they are in the presence of God? Do our lives and our presence transfigure their lives or disfigure the face of God?

How do we look at people? What do we really see? Each human being, because of the mystery of the Incarnation and the Eucharist, is incorporated into the body of Christ. Do we see the glory of God shining through them? Do we see through them, their bodies and their outward appearances, to the heart of God? Especially do we look at those who suffer among us, those who suffer because of injustice and sin, those who suffer unjustly and innocently as the Crucified One in our midst? The mystery of the cross that Jesus preaches transfigures all of reality if we but have the eyes of faith and obedience to see what God is doing in our world and among all of us all the time. In a sense, at baptism we are given glory-eyes so that we can see the way God sees. We are told to look at people with eyes of love, of forgiveness and reconciliation, and see them all as God sees them.

We are called to pray, to dwell consciously in the presence of God so that our eyes are washed out again and again so that we can see clearly, through the eyes of faith, the eyes of the Word, the eyes of the Spirit, the eyes of Truth, and look upon all with the eyes of compassion, the eyes of God. How well do we see? Are we praying with Jesus, with the Scriptures of the law, the prophets, and the Word of God made flesh among us, in community? And are we listening to that Word so that we can get past our fears and all the din of the world around us telling us the exact opposite of what Jesus teaches and commands that we do. Or are we, sadly, like his disciples, turning from him, resisting some of his words and teachings as too hard, too demanding, too naive, too idealistic, too dangerous for us to put into practice? Are we listening to Jesus with one ear and to the world with the other? And so, are we looking at some people with our glory-eyes and some with the eyes of the world?

The Transfiguration is more than a moment. It is a way of living, of seeing and acting because we believe. By baptism we have been transfigured into the body of

Christ that we share at Eucharist. The radiant face of God is shining through every human being all the time, and our lives are to be those of disciples, practicing here and now on everyone so that we might one day see the fullness of God shining on the face of Jesus and on everyone. We must make sure that the faces and eyes of all who meet us, know us, and know the consequences of our actions and words glisten with the glory of hope and catch a glimpse of the glory of God shining through us. And we must look at each face in the world with great care, so that we can see through it the glory of God.

We are called by Jesus to transfigure the world we live in and to bring the glory of God to the places and situations that are most in need of glory, of hope, and the presence of God. The places of war, destruction, hopelessness and despair, of violence and abuse, of injustice, greed, avarice and lies, of natural resources stolen and used for death—these are where we are commanded to bring radiance and transfiguration. We are to transfigure the hard news of the world into the Good News of God. And to do this, we must pray. The disciples are given a glimpse of how Jesus dwells in his inner world and spirit with God. And where he dwells with his Father, you will find the prophets, the liberators, the lawgivers—those who are faithful to the covenant speaking the truth about the hard places of life, places of passover, and places where life is threatened and death looms. Prayer is for Jesus in this moment of transfiguration, about facing death and the hope of resurrection; about facing rejection and terror, the cross and brutality, at the hands of others with dignity, with the freedom that is given to a child of God and with the glory of God within that sustains, strengthens, and gives courage in the face of these horrors human beings can inflict upon one another. John of the Cross and Teresa of Ávila, who were such good friends of God, have both had this statement attributed to them: "You must pray as though everything depended on God, but you must work as though everything depended on you."

There is a marvelous Jewish story that speaks simply about what it means to live a life that is transfigured. Once upon a time the prophet Elijah visited a very holy rabbi. The rabbi was surprised to see Elijah in his study and even more so when Elijah told him that God was pleased with him and he could have any gift that he'd like but he had to decide right then and there. The rabbi was flustered but he blurted out, "Do you think I could have a glimpse of Paradise? It would make it so much easier to live here on earth where there is so much pain and injustice if I could see it just this once." And in a flash Elijah and the rabbi were standing inside the gates of heaven. The rabbi was floored—it was beyond description. Lovely, radiance permeating everything. He was speechless.

But as he looked around, he became dismayed and said to Elijah, "There's hardly anyone here! Don't tell me that after all these years there are so few that made it into Paradise? Where are all the saints, the holy ones?" Elijah looked at him and responded, "Rabbi, you of all people should know—the saints aren't in Paradise, Paradise is in the saints! Oh, they come here, some of them, but they usually opt to return to earth so they can see the glory of God everywhere. Once you know that God's glory resides in every human being and in some more than others, well, you go looking for it everywhere." And in another flash, the rabbi was back in his study, alone. He stood there for a long time pondering what he had seen, heard, and learned. And then he thought to himself: What in the world do people see when they look at me? Do they see that Paradise is within me and marvel at the glory of God shining on my face? And then, he thought again: How do I see all the people in my life, in the world? Do I see the glory of God radiantly shining on their faces? O God, have pity on me, on us all, and give me eyes to perceive your glory among us.

Let us pray. "Jesus, the mystery of your Transfiguration tells us to look through you to see God and to listen only to your words so that we clearly hear the voice of God. May we learn from you how to pray and to practice seeing the glory of God radiantly shining on the faces of all the children of God, made lovingly in your image. May we never disfigure any of the faces and bodies of your children, or the earth that you have made that reflects the light of your goodness. May we live our lives so that your own Spirit, your glory, comes shining through us, bringing light and hope to others, especially those living in the face of suffering, death, injustice, violence, and fear, as you did when you were on earth.

And may we listen to you when you speak of the cross and death and resurrection and not be dismayed by our own fears. Instead may we turn and look at you with confidence and awe, knowing that you walk with us and we are to fall in behind you on the way to glory. May your Father's glory come shining through us this day and every day until we see your glory face-to-face. We ask this, with you, in the name of our Father and your Holy Spirit. Amen."

THE FIFTH MYSTERY OF THE LIGHT:

The Eucharist

SCRIPTURE

It was before the feast of the Passover, Jesus realized that his hour had come to pass from this world to the Father, and as he had loved those who were his own in the world, he would love them with perfect love.

They were at supper and the devil had already put into the mind of Judas, son of Simon Iscariot, to betray Jesus. Jesus knew that the Father had entrusted all things to him, and as he had come from God he was going to God. So he got up from the table, removed his garment and taking a towel, wrapped it around his waist. Then he poured water into a basin and began to wash his disciples' feet and to wipe them with the towel he was wearing.

When he came to Simon Peter, Simon said to him, "Why, Lord, do you want to wash my feet?" Jesus said, "What I am doing you cannot understand now, but afterwards you will understand it." Peter replied, "You shall never wash my feet."

Jesus answered him, "If I do not wash you, you can have no part with me." Then Simon Peter said, "Lord, wash not only my feet, but also my hands and my head!"

Jesus replied, "Whoever has taken a bath does not need to wash (except the feet), for he is clean all over. You are clean, though not all of you." Jesus knew who was to betray him: because of this he said, "Not all of you are clean."

When Jesus had finished washing their feet, he put on his garment again, went back to the table and said to them, "Do you understand what I have done to you? You call me Master and Lord, and you are right, for so I am. If I, then, your Lord and Master, have washed your feet you also must wash one another's feet. I have just given you an example that as I have done, so you must do."

Truly I say to you, the servant is not greater than his master, nor is the messenger greater than he who sent him. Understand this, and blessed are you if you put it into practice.

Or,

When the hour came, Jesus took his place at table and the apostles with him. And he said to them, "I was eager to eat this passover with you before I suffer; for, I tell you, I shall not eat it again until it is fulfilled in the kingdom of God." Then they passed him a cup and when he had given thanks he said, "Take this and share it among yourselves. For I tell you that from now on I will not drink of the grape of the wine until the kingdom of God comes." Jesus also took bread, and after giving thanks, he broke it and gave it to them saying, "This is my body which is given for you. Do this in remembrance of me." And he did the same with the cup after eating, "This cup is the new covenant, sealed in my blood which is poured out for you." (Luke 22:14–20)

Or Mark 14:17–25, or Matthew 26:20–29.

> "Next to the Blessed Sacrament itself, your neighbor is the holiest object presented to your senses."
>
> —C. S. LEWIS,
> "WEIGHT OF GLORY"

This fifth mystery of light is the "institution of the Eucharist in which Christ offers his body and blood as food under the signs of bread and wine, and testifies 'to the end' his love for humanity (John 13:1), for whose salvation he will offer himself in sacrifice." (RVM, #21) With these words John Paul II chooses to emphasize the depth and extent of Jesus' love for us in staying with us in the Eucharist. But in choosing the reflection from John's gospel, he also is emphasizing not just the insitution of the Eucharist, which is found in Mark, Matthew, and Luke, but the story of Jesus washing the feet of his disciples, unique to John, who depicts Jesus at the Last Supper but has no story of the actual institution of the Eucharist as a meal. Instead there is the modeling of how to do and be the Eucharist with our whole persons and our lives, in service to one another, imitating our Lord and Master.

Luke's account of the last supper Jesus shares with his friends begins with Jesus telling them how much he has longed to eat this Passover with them, or how much he has "desired" to share this Passover "with you before I suffer." This is important because the word used is *epithumia*, one of the four words used in Greek to mean "love" (the others being *eros, philia,* and *agape*). *Epithumia* usually means the desire of a woman to give birth to a child. It has a sense of future, of hope and wonderment, but also of the unknown, and a sense of urgency and need. Jesus desires to share the Passover ritual meal with his friends before he suffers. Both the meal, when he transforms the ritual of the Passover into the Eucharist, and his suffering and death are bound intimately together. Eucharist is both a meal and a sacrifice that gives birth to a new covenant, a new community, a new way of worshiping God, a new way of sharing in the presence of God, and a new way of being one with God. There is the sense that this night, this last supper, is one of joy and great longing and hope, but also dread, fear, and anguish at what lies ahead for him.

In John's gospel, after Jesus has washed his disciples feet and goes to recline at table, he speaks of many things to his friends. He warns them of what is coming and uses this image of a woman in childbirth to describe himself and what will happen when the meal is over and they leave to go to the garden, where his passion and death, his travail and work of passover, will begin in his own flesh and blood. The meal where he leaves bread and wine as his presence becomes sacrifice where his body and blood are given over into our hands as surely as he handed the bread and cup around to his disciples. He tells them: "Truly, I say to you, you will weep and mourn while the world rejoices. You will be sorrowful, but your sorrow will turn to joy. A woman in childbirth is in distress because her time is at hand. But after the child is born, she no longer remembers her suffering because of such great joy: a human being is born into the world." (John 16:20–21)

Jesus himself will pass through the experience of giving birth to his community, his church, and will feel both the ecstastic joy and the wrenching pain that accompanies this dying and birthing process. And afterward there will be no remembrance of the pain, only the joy at what has come into the world—a human being. Jesus tells his disciples and us "to do this in remembrance of me." He is speaking about the Eucharist, the ritual of the new covenant of his life and death, his body and blood. He is telling us to take hold of our lives and all we hold dear (bread) and give thanks to God for them, and break them up, hand them over in sacrifice, and share them with all the world. This is the ritual that marks our living. It gathers all of our lives and takes them to the altar/table and makes of them and our bodies the body and blood of Christ. What happens to the bread and wine—the transformation into the body and blood of Christ—also happens to our bodies and lives: we become transformed into the body and blood of Christ. We become what we eat and then go out into the world to be bread for the world and wine for hope and courage so that all may come to know and give glory to God because of the way we live our lives.

But he is also saying "Do *this* in remembrance of me," do what I do when I bend before all of you and wash your feet, do all the things that I have done to serve those in need and be a servant who gives his life as a ransom for the many. The disciples are reluctant to have Jesus bend before them as a common slave or household servant, to take off their sandals and wash their very dirty feet (from traveling the dusty roads and streets littered with refuse). But Jesus wants them and us to know that we are to bend before one another in respect, in regard, and to see one another in this light.

The story is finely crafted and the words carefully chosen. Jesus rises from the table and lays aside his garment, washes their feet, and then takes up his garment again. This is the same phrase that is used when he speaks earlier of "laying down his life and taking it up again," when he speaks of being the Good Shepherd who lays down his life for his sheep.

> I am the good shepherd. The good shepherd gives his life [lays down his life] for the sheep. . . . I am the good shepherd. I know my own and my own know me, as the Father knows me and I know the Father. Because of this I give my life [lay down my life] for my sheep.
>
> The Father loves me because I lay down my life in order to take it up again. No one takes it from me, but I lay it down freely. It is mine to lay down and to take up again: this mission I received from my Father. (John 10:11, 14–15, 17–18)

Jesus' laying down of his life has been what he has done all his life. His mission from his Father has been to be servant to us, to bend before us, and it culminates in his giving his very life so that we might have life, ever more abundantly. This is a way of living, an example of a lifestyle and an attitude toward others. It is service, cleansing, restoration, humility, and love. It is Jesus' vocation and our own vocation, and the Father loves Jesus for this life that he lives and lays down on behalf of others. The Father loves us when we too live as servants and lay down our lives for one another in love.

This same verb phrasing is used again in the Acts of the Apostles, in describing how the community lived together, sharing all things in common so that there was no poor among them: "There was no needy person among them, for those who owned land or houses, sold them and brought the proceeds of the sale. And they laid it at the feet of the apostles who distributed it according to each one's need." (Acts 4:34–35)

The pattern of the words of doing the Eucharist in community as our worship ritual, and the pattern of the words of how to live in community so that there is no one in need among us, are almost the same: take, give thanks, break/share/lay down, and distribute to others. What we do with the bread and wine of our lives, we are to do with all the other resources of our lives. We give it all, along with our bodies and souls, in gratitude to the Father for the immeasurable gift of Jesus and Jesus' Spirit, given to transform our lives. This requires of us a most uncommon, daring, and audacious faith, to respond to Jesus' words and example laid before us on this last night before he died.

A friend of mine from the Middle East was telling me some remarkable things about bread one day while we were eating. We were eating his style, not Western style, and it was most likely the way Jesus and his contemporaries ate too. He said, "Bread is everything to us. It's not something extra that you serve on the side at a meal. It's the core of our meal. It's even our way of eating, our utensils. We have pita bread, pocket bread, and we break off a piece of bread and use it to pick up the rest of our food and we eat with it. Whenever anyone else wants to taste something, we break off a piece of our bread, use it to pick up another kind of food, and feed the other person with it—not handing it to them, but usually putting it, with the bread, into their mouths. The only way to get to the other food is with the bread. We rarely use forks and knives, only when Westerners are present, and they are awkward with the way we eat together." To think of this in relation to Jesus, who calls himself the Bread of Life, is stunning. He's saying the only way you can really live is to live in him, and with him, and through him. This is our Eucharist, our worship, and our way of life. None of us can live without this bread of life! But once we have eaten, then we become the body of Christ, and our lives are food and drink, sustenance and encouragement, for everyone who is hungry.

John Kavanaugh wrote once when speaking about the eucharistic meaning of the parable of the sheep and goats that when Jesus equates himself with "the least of our brothers and sisters," he somehow effected a second "transubstantiation." Just as the bread and wine become the body and blood of Christ, so too have the least among us become the body and blood of Christ. "Christ has said over the least of us: 'This is my body.' " ("The Word," *America*, May 28, 1994) And he goes on to say:

> When we labor for human rights, when we shelter the poor, when we dismantle the bombs, when we protect the unborn, when we reach out to the criminal, we do these things not as political ac-

tivists or social workers. We do them not as liber-
als or conservatives. We do them as people who
worship the incarnate God. The body and blood
of Christ is not only our redemption. It is our
task.

This is our work, our service, our feet-washing that Jesus
has modeled for us in his own works, as he obeys his
Father's mission.

Jesus speaks of the wine at the supper and says that he
will not drink of it again until the kingdom comes into
the world. In the prayer of the Our Father, we pray "may
your kingdom come, your will be done" before we even
ask God "to give us today the bread we need." In a real way
the Eucharist is the sacrament of the kingdom of God
among us. We celebrate the kingdom, where all are fed,
all share in the goodness of God, and all are satisfied and
learn to love those who hunger for justice, for truth, and
for peace on earth. Jesus gives us his body in bread and
wine and then gives his body in crucifixion, so that the
kingdom of forgiveness, mercy and justice, and peace
may come upon earth. The Eucharist is the kingdom
sacrament and we celebrate it so that we might have the
courage to bring that kingdom daily into the world by our
service and work, in obedience to Jesus' own words and
life. When we receive the Eucharist and the cup from the
hands of other disciples who pass it to us, we say, "the
body of Christ," "the blood of Christ," but we could also
say "The kingdom of God is close at hand: repent and

believe the Good News." And we would all answer resoundingly, "Amen."

In John Paul II's recent letter on the Eucharist, *"Ecclesia de Eucharistia,"* he quotes many of the early theologians of the church that connect the Eucharist not only to Jesus' passion and death but also to his Resurrection. The connections give much food for reflection and integration into our spirituality and practice of our faith.

> It is as the living and risen One that Christ can become in the Eucharist, the "bread of life" (John 6:35, 48), the "living bread" (John 6:51). Saint Ambrose reminded the newly initiated that the Eucharist applies the event of the resurrection to their lives: "Today Christ is yours, yet each day he rises again for you." Saint Cyril of Alexandria also makes clear that sharing in the sacred mysteries "is a true confession and a remembrance that the Lord died and returned to life for us and on our behalf." (RVM, #14–20)

In this same section John Paul II quotes from Paul in his letter to the Corinthians and reminds the Church that from the beginning, it made them "unworthy" to partake of the Lord's Supper "amid division and indifference towards the poor" (cf. 1 Corinthians 11:17–22, 27–34). And he ends this section on the Eucharist as the mystery of our faith with these words:

Proclaiming the death of the Lord "until he comes" (1 Corinthians 11:26) entails that all who take part in the Eucharist must be committed to changing their lives and making them in a certain way completely "Eucharistic." It is this fruit of a transfigured existence and a commitment to transforming the world in accordance with the Gospel which splendidly illustrates the eschatological tension inherent in the celebration of the Eucharist and in the Christian life as a whole. "Come, Lord Jesus!" (Revelation 22:20) (RVM, #21)

Let us pray. "Lord, your last gift to us was your own body and blood in the Eucharist, your presence among us as food and drink. You gave your life, your body, and your love so that we could live on your words, your flesh, your heart, and your food. You have told us to 'do this in remembrance of you.' May we do this: celebrate Eucharist and feast with you, on your words, your presence, your bread and wine, given for us. May we do this: feed all the hungry, heal, and bring life to those who lack what they need to live ever more abundantly. May we do this: bring courage and hope, the reality of your kingdom of justice and peace to every situation and every place where violence and injustice seem to prevail. May we do this: remember you and tell your stories of forgiveness and mercy, offering reconciliation and restoring wholeness in your name. May we become what we eat, your body and blood, and go out into the world so that those who hunger and thirst for your justice and peace, your presence in their lives, may find it in us. May we remember the words of one of your early disciples: 'It is a far, far better thing to feed the hungry than it is to raise the dead.' May there be no one who goes hungry in this world while we celebrate your presence among us as food for life and our way home. We ask this, O Lord, in the name of the Father and the Son and the Spirit. Amen."

FIVE

The Sorrowful Mysteries

"It's not over yet!"

—BRENDAN LOVETT

THESE FEW words "It's not over yet!" is a
book title reflecting upon the events of
Holy Week, by Brendan Lovett. The title is based on a series of paintings by a
German artist, Roland Peter Litzen-
burger, that appears in the book. He
chose the name for the series because he
wanted to make it clear that "the Passion
of Jesus is to be placed within the ongoing story of the passion of humankind,
in solidarity with the suffering people of

all times and places. It cannot be understood apart from this wider ongoing story." (From the Introduction, Manila, Philippines: Claretian Publications, 1999)

Traditionally the Stations of the Cross, a Lenten devotion, focus on specific moments leading up to and including the death of Jesus by crucifixion. John Paul II, in his statement on the sorrowful mysteries, writes that in these individual moments of Jesus' suffering and death "are found the culmination of the revelation of God's love and the source of our salvation. The Rosary selects certain moments from the passion, inviting the faithful to contemplate them in their hearts and to relive them." (RVM, #22) It is in reflecting on these experiences of Jesus' own terrible sufferings that we begin to become sensitized to the sufferings of others and commit ourselves to changing the world. To be human is to suffer, but too much suffering is not a result of the natural causes of aging, or illness, or facing life's inevitable hardships. Far too much suffering is the effect of injustice, of violence, of sin and evil that human beings do to one another, and it is imperative for believers in the Crucified and Risen Lord to do everything in their power to eliminate and to relieve these forms of suffering—to lift the burden of the cross from other people's lives. Now we are invited to walk with Jesus, our Crucified Lord, through his passion, all the way to the cross, and on to resurrection's glory.

❀ THE FIRST SORROWFUL MYSTERY:

The Agony in the Garden

SCRIPTURE

After this, Jesus left to go as usual to Mount Olive
and the disciples followed him. When he came to
the place, he told them, "Pray that you may not be
put to the test." Then he went a little farther,
about a stone's throw, and kneeling down he
prayed, "Father, if it is your will, remove this cup
from me; still not my will but yours be done."
And an angel from heaven appeared to give him
strength.

As he was in agony, he prayed even more
earnestly and great drops of blood formed like
sweat and fell to the ground. When he rose from
prayer, he went to his disciples but found them
worn out with grief, and asleep. And he said to
them, "Why do you sleep? Get up and pray, so
that you may not be put to the test."

Jesus was still speaking when a group appeared and the man named Judas, one of the
Twelve, was leading them. He drew near to Jesus
to kiss him, and Jesus said to him, "Did you need
this kiss to betray the Son of Man?" (Luke
22:39–48)

Or,

They came to a place which was called Gethsemane and Jesus said to his disciples, "Sit here while I pray." But he took Peter, James and John along with him, and becoming filled with fear and distress, he said to them, "My soul is full of sorrow, even to death. Remain here and stay awake." Then he went a little further on and fell to the ground, praying that if possible this hour might pass him by. Jesus said, "Abba, all things are possible for you; take this cup away from me. Yet not what I want, but what you want."

Then he came and found them asleep and said to Peter, "Simon, are you sleeping? Keep watch and pray, all of you, so that you may not slip into temptation. The spirit indeed is eager but human nature is weak." And going away he prayed saying the same words. When he came back to the disciples, he found them asleep again; they could not keep their eyes open, and they did not know what to say to him.

When he came back a third time, he said, "You can sleep on now and take your rest! It is all over, the time has come; the Son of Man is now given into the hands of sinners. Get up, let us go. Look: the one betraying me is right here."(Mark 14:32–42)

Or, Matthew 26:36–46.

"Here I am, Lord God, I come to do your will."

—PSALM 40:7–8

The turning of Jesus toward Jerusalem, where all the prophets have confronted the sin of the people and their leaders and where they all met with suffering and death, begins in a garden. It is a place of anguish, where Jesus offers a fervent prayer for release and yet just as fervent a prayer for the courage to continue living so as to die with faithfulness to the will of God, and integrity as a human being intent on obedience to God's Word. It is a place of acceptance and determination and pure worship of God the Father. Sadly, it is also a place of betrayal and stark aloneness as Jesus confronts the bitterness of being left by his disciples to face the treachery of the religious and political authorities alone. And perhaps the hardest of all is the moment when one of his own disciples, whom he has called his friend, betrays him for thirty pieces of silver and a kiss publicly declaring his devotion and privately tearing at the heart of his master, Jesus.

Jesus begins to face what will happen to him at the hands of "sinners," all human beings, by going, as is his custom, to pray in the evening. He invites his disciples to come along with him, and specifically singles out Peter, James, and John to accompany him even more closely, as once he did when he invited them up the mountain to be witnesses to his transfiguration in glory as he prayed to his Father. He is inviting them to pray with him, but also to accompany him in his passion; to walk the way of the cross with him. But they cannot; they will not. In the beginning they are overcome with grief, an intimation that something terrible is about to happen, perhaps gleaned from Jesus' words at their supper. And they are overcome with exhaustion and sleep, escaping from having to immediately face what they are sensing about this night and what it may bring to pass.

They succumb to weariness, even though they are asked to pray with him. The description of sleep often means unawareness and the inability to know what is happening. The disciples have been resisting much of what Jesus has been trying to tell them about his coming betrayal, rejection by the chief priests and religious leaders of the people, false accusations, torture, and execution by crucifixion at the hands of the Romans. They have been blocking it out—this just can't happen to their Master and this just cannot be what will become of their dreams and hopes for Jesus and their own rise in his kingdom.

It is only Jesus who faces the darkness, seeking his Father and intimacy with him. Jesus is a Jew, steeped in the psalms, prayers, and laments of his people, and as he bows before God, he most assuredly falls back on the prayers that he has always said in difficulty, rejection, and disappointment as he has traveled and preached the Good News of God to the poor. Psalm 40 echoes precisely what Jesus faces on this last night before others come to destroy him and seek to put an end to his words and his life. He prays:

> With resolve I waited for the Lord; he listened and heard me beg.
> Out of the horrid pit he drew me, out of deadly quicksand. He
> settled my feet upon a rock and made my steps steady.

He put a new song into my mouth, a song of praise to our God.
Many will see and be awed and put their trust in the Lord.

Blessed is the one who relies on the Lord and does not look to the
proud nor go astray after false gods.

How numerous, O Lord, are your wonderful deeds! In your
marvellous plans for us you are beyond compare! How many
they are—I cannot tell them or count their number.

Sacrifice and oblation you did not desire; this you had me
understand.

Burnt offering and sin offering you do not require.

Then I said, "Here I come! as the scroll says of me. To do your will
is my delight, O God, for your law is within my heart."

In the great assembly I have proclaimed your saving help. My lips,
O Lord, I did not seal—you know that very well.

I have not locked up in my heart your saving help, but have spoken
about it—your deliverance and your faithfulness;

I have made no secret of your truth and your kindness in the great
assembly.

Do not withhold from me, O Lord, your mercy; let your love and
faithfulness preserve me constantly.

For troubles beyond number have closed in on me; I am all covered
by sins and I cannot see. They are more than the hairs of my
head, and I am losing courage.

May it please you, O Lord, to rescue me. Make haste, O Lord, to
help me!

May those who seek my life be brought to shame and disgrace; may
those who want me destroyed be turned back in confusion.

May those who taunt me with "Aha, aha!" be filled with shame
and consternation.

*But may all those who seek you rejoice and be glad in you; and may
all who love your saving grace continually say, "The Lord is
great."*
*Though I am afflicted and poor, yet the Lord thinks of me. You are
my help and my savior—O Lord, do not delay!*

This psalm describes Jesus' own life and teaching and
situation in the garden perfectly, and would have been on
his lips and in his heart, as he poured out his soul before
God. He reached for understanding, for escape from the
horrors that the night and the following day would bring
him, and for the courage to face his death with grace, with
human dignity, and with God's courage and steadfast-
ness. He knows the degrading humiliation and inhuman
suffering that is planned as part of the crucifixion ritual.
The Romans devised this torture to make a public statement about anyone who would stand in opposition to the
empire's rule. They sought to deter those who would follow in the footsteps of an insurgent and a terrorist by
making a spectacle of their leader's death. Jesus knows
that from the moment the push to execution begins, he
will know no mercy from anyone involved in the process.
And so he falls before his Father seeking mercy.

Jesus is human and so he must die. But he did not
have to die so terribly. This was the decision of many
people who were fearful of Jesus preaching and the hope
he gave to so many without hope of a life beyond the
sheer struggle to survive day to day under oppression
and slavery. Many participated in the actual carrying-out

of the order to crucify him, but many others participated in collusion with the death decree. And still others participated in Jesus' sufferings by false witness, by letting the crowd carry them along with insults, curses, and taunts. Worse still, his own followers and so many that he had healed, forgiven, and given new life to participated in his sufferings by abandoning him to the crowd and the authorities. They had been invited to stand with him as friends and followers, in gratitude for what he had done for them and in faithfulness to him and his Word. Jesus prayed that they would be with him in his suffering and death, but all refused and all ran, protecting their own lives and leaving Jesus to the rage and violence of the mob and the leaders set on protecting their own small domains.

Jesus steels his will to face torture and death by crucifixion, and his body rebels and trembles at the fear and pain that he will be subject to in the many hours that lie before him. He has heard the murmurs of the crowd and the turmoil of the people and knows that it is a matter of time before they move on him. He could have left the city. He could have slipped away, but he stands his ground and remains. But Jesus is the Truth. And his words are about life, life that is stronger than death, stronger than hate and evil, and so he will stand before hate and sin, stand before suffering and death that is born of evil, and remain faithful to God. Jesus rises from his prayer, believing that his Father is still with him and will be with him to the very end. He looks with great sadness on his friends, who will not be faithful and who will desert him. Jesus is human and so enters into the pain and suffering of every human being, taking it into his body and soul as he gathers his life and his love for God and for all of us and turns to face those who would silence him and kill him. He rouses his disciples because they are about to set upon him like animals on a hunt to the death.

This is not the will of God. The will of God is always about life. This is sin and the evil men and women do to one another in violence, misusing power and attacking others with hate. The will of God is Jesus standing in his humanness and with the grace of God as others approach him, intent on destroying him. The will of God in Jesus is vulnerable and fearful, but faithful and true. Even though Jesus' Father has remained silent and no sign of comfort is given to him, Jesus believes and leans on his Father for the strength to face all the hate and evil coming toward him. He is the man of sorrows, suffering as much at the hands of human beings as he suffers for the insult to God the creator and lover of all humankind, when humans distort what it means to be created in the image of God who is Father, calling us his beloved children and sharing with us his own Spirit of forgiveness and justice. It is time to stand with Jesus and face the evil and sufferings of the world and to remain with him as he invites us to pray with him.

Let us pray. "Jesus, you invite us always to come and pray with you to the Father in your own Spirit of truth. You ask us to be faithful and to remain with you in the face of sorrow, of suffering, of persecution, of torture and death. You remind us that you are with us through everything that happens to us and that you are close no matter what the world, its governments and authorities, or other human beings do to us. And you ask us to stand with you, giving testimony to your Word of Truth and your command of love, of compassion, and accompaniment with those who suffer, especially those who suffer like you, unjustly at the hands of others. Jesus, this time and always, may we remain awake, pray with you, and stay close in faithfulness to you and all those who suffer because of the sin and evil of others or because they speak the truth on behalf of the world. We pray with you: 'Here I am, O God, I come to do your will and to bring life to all.' Amen."

THE SECOND SORROWFUL MYSTERY:

The Scourging of Jesus

SCRIPTURES

As Pilate wanted to please the people, he freed Barabbas and after the flogging of Jesus had him handed over to be crucified. (Mark 15:15)

Or,

Then Pilate had Jesus taken away and scourged. The soldiers also twisted thorns into a crown and put it on his head. They threw a cloak of royal purple around his shoulders and began coming up to him and saluting him, "Hail, king of the Jews," and struck him on the face.

Pilate went outside yet another time and said to the Jews, "Look, I am bringing him out and I want you to know that I find no crime in him." Jesus then came out wearing the crown of thorns and the purple cloak and Pilate pointed to him saying, "Here is the man!" (*Ecce homo!*) (John 19:1–5)

> *I live each day to kill death;*
> *I die each day to beget life,*
> *and in this dying unto death,*
> *I die a thousand times and*
> *am reborn another thousand*
> *through that love.*
>
> —JULIA ESQUIVEL

This sorrowful moment skips from the betrayal with Judas's kiss in the garden and passes over the long night that leads to Jesus' being brought before Pilate. Once Jesus is arrested by a crowd of soldiers that belonged to the high priest's army, paid mercenaries and bystanders who had gone along to see what would happen, he is brought to the courtyard of the house of the high priest, where the leaders had been assembled hastily to find evidence to convict Jesus in the religious court. False witnesses are brought in and they contradict themselves in their testimonies. Jesus is interrogated by the high priest and speaks truthfully about who he is and what he preaches. He steadfastly refuses to deny who he is, saying that he is the Son of Man, a prophet of God, and a judge of the people. (Mark 14:60–64) They use his own words, twisting them to declare him worthy of death. Then in anger, rage, and hate, they turn on him. The gospel writes: "Some of them began to spit on Jesus and, blindfolding him, they struck him saying, 'Play the prophet!' And the guards set upon him with blows." (Mark 14:65)

The trial is a mockery, a formality that must be attended to before they can approach Pilate, the territorial governor, and ask him to make a formal decree of death by crucifixion. As leaders of a nation occupied by the Romans, they had no authority to put someone to death.

Jesus is abused physically and verbally throughout the night. It is only with the light of day that they drag him before Pilate, seeking the sentence of death to be carried out legally. Everything must be done legally, while seeming to be the right thing to do, with murderous intent from the beginning. Pilate has Jesus brought before him, to interrogate him. But Pilate senses that Jesus has done nothing to merit death by crucifixion, and that he has been handed over to him because of jealousy and fear. He does not want to get involved and tries one tactic after another to deter the Sanhedrin from their intent to have Jesus killed. He offers them a political prisoner, a terrorist who has attacked a Roman garrison, in his stead, using a custom of freeing someone the people want freed to derail them. But the whole affair has been orchestrated and the people cry out for Barabbas instead, and Pilate is caught in his own plan and must release Barabbas instead of Jesus. But before Jesus will be led to his execution by crucifixion by the Roman soldiers under his command, he follows the usual prelude to death by having Jesus scourged.

In the Gospels, this act of scourging, the second sorrowful mystery, is covered in one or two lines, with no description of what actually happened and what Jesus would have experienced in this torture. Usually there were thirty-nine blows with a whip, fashioned of rawhide or leather, splayed into as many as ten pieces tipped with iron or glass. It was unnecessary, torture for the pure sake of inflicting pain and humiliation, an attempt to reduce a person to a mass of open, torn wounds that were inches deep, flaying skin from the body. It was military torture, a bone thrown to the soldiers to play with prior to the gruesome and brutal killing of a person in public, hard work that they were used to doing under the hateful eyes of the people who depised them for their presence in their country, let alone the killing they did as invaders and occupiers.

Tradition tells us that Jesus is taken into the praetorium, the gathering place of the soldiers and officers, an inner sanctum, and insulted, humiliated, stripped naked, bound to a low pillar, and flogged.

This mystery, perhaps more clearly than any other,

reeks of evil and hate, of violence and hostility that human beings can direct toward another person, making him a victim of rage and brutality. This mystery demands that we look at evil that is not just what one person does to another, but what systems, nations, governments, organizations, groups, armies, those in authority, and those with power do as reprisal to those who resist the evil and injustice that they inflict upon the world. And it seems that when the victim who is tortured does not retaliate with cursing, rage, and mutual hate, but remains human, it makes those who inflict the suffering rage even more. Being human in the face of inhumanity evokes violence and murder. Just being human condemns what is being done, and instead of causing shame, it evokes more fury and intent to destroy what is good and holy in the one who is being made to suffer.

This is the torture inflicted upon Jesus by the Roman soldiers, just part of the job of killing those who would stand in opposition to what the empire built on military power; conquest of nations, cultures, religions, and peoples; aggression and domination; greed; and even the making of gods out of their leaders demanded. And Jesus, though torn to shreds, literally, retains his sense of being human, being every person made in the image of God, in spite of what others do to destroy that image and deny life to all people. This mystery demands that we look at and know this evil as still rampant in the world, in every country and government, including our own, and not to ignore what is done in the name of security, protection, safety, and national sovereignty around the world. Jesus' kingdom is in this world but it does not use power as other kingdoms do. Jesus' power is found in meekness—another word for nonviolence—in forgiveness for anyone who does evil, calling him to the truth and repentance, and by refusing to respond to any action with injustice or evil that would harm another. There is in evil a rage that responds to this kind of truth and goodness with ever-increasing brutality and inhumanity. Even if we do not commit these acts of brutality ourselves often we are part of nations and people that allow them to continue without resistance or calling attention to them. We do evil and are in collusion with such grave sin and mortal killing of the human spirit and human bodies.

Decades ago Huub Oosterhuis wrote a prayer that haunts and tells us the truth about who we are and what destroying Jesus and others physically says about us. As hard as this actual moment of torture is—both in regards to Jesus' own body and so many others treated in the same way over the centuries—we must look at what we are capable of doing and what we actually do to one another and think that we can see regarding ourselves as human beings: "Lord God, we see the sins of the world in the light of your only son. Since his coming to be your mercy toward us we have come to suspect how hard and unrelenting we are toward each other. . . ." (*Your Word Is Near.* New York: Newman Press, 1968, p. 131)

Once again, this mystery of Jesus, human among us and yet Son of God, demands that we decide where we stand and who we stand with: do we stand with Jesus and with all those tortured, abused, humiliated, dehumanized, and physically destroyed by those with power and violence, or do we stand with those who obey the systems and demands of the world—armies, governments, nations, those who enforce laws that though deemed legal are unjust and inhuman, and those who in rage wreak destruction on other human persons, beloved by God? If we cringe in horror and are sympathetic to Jesus as he is scourged then we must commit ourselves to stopping such horror and working for human rights for all people everywhere.

Let us pray. "Jesus, you are handed over to be sacrificed to those whose lives are controlled by violence and anger. You stand helpless, fearful, and terrified at what is done to you, suffering innocently at the hands of those who are cowardly, acting in groups that validate the evil they do as necessary, or who take pleasure in the pain of others that they victimize. Lord, you are attacked, like so many in our world, by those who decide to do evil that escalates into murder. Jesus, we are afraid of such suffering and of other human beings who can do such harm. Help us to resist this kind of evil in our world, remembering your sufferings, and to do everything we can together as your children to alleviate the pain of people so victimized around the world. Jesus, scourged and torn apart with violence, teach us to live with courage and to do no harm to anyone, ever. We ask this in your name, Jesus. Amen."

THE THIRD SORROWFUL MYSTERY:

Jesus Crowned with Thorns

SCRIPTURE

The soldiers took him inside the courtyard known as the praetorium and called the rest of their companions. They clothed him in a purple cloak and twisting a crown of thorns, they forced it onto his head. Then they began saluting him, "Long life to the King of the Jews!" With a stick they gave him blows on the head and spat on him; then they knelt down pretending to worship him.

When they had finished mocking him, they pulled off the purple cloak and put his own clothes on him. (Mark 15:16–20a)

Or,

Then Pilate had Jesus taken away and scourged. The soldiers also twisted thorns into a crown and put it on his head. They threw a cloak of royal purple around his shoulders and began coming up to him and saluting him, "Hail, king of the Jews," and they struck him on the face.

Pilate went outside yet another time and said to the Jews, "Look, I am bringing him out and I want you to know that I find no crime in him." Jesus then came out wearing the crown of thorns and the purple cloak and Pilate pointed to him, saying, "Here is the man!" (John 19:1–5)

*"Ecce Homo! Behold the Man! The Lord is cast
into the most abject suffering."*

—JOHN PAUL II

Jesus is God's sign of contradiction that paradoxically
blesses us in his life and sufferings and death. It is Pilate
who speaks the words, *"Ecce Homo!"* Behold the man! Look
at him! And Jesus stands broken in body, silent before a
mob, bleeding, his skin hanging from him, shaking in
uncontrollable reaction to torturous pain, stared at and
looked at with disdain. John Paul II writes in his description of the sorrowful mysteries about the depth of meaning found in these words, but found in the person of
Jesus in his pain: "This abject suffering reveals not only
the love of God but also the meaning of man himself.
Ecce Homo: the meaning, origin and fulfillment of man
is to be found in Christ, the God who humbles himself
out of love 'even unto death, death on a cross.' "
(Philippians 2:8) (RVM, #22)

This mystery says that our God suffers with us, for us,
in us, and through us and that our lives are only lived with
God, for God, in God, and through God. There is so
much blood and misery in these mysteries and especially
in the mystery of the scourging and crowning with
thorns. The mysteries of the crucifixion and death of
Jesus are more than statements about personal sin and
evil: they are statements about the nature of evil and how
it pervades and corrodes structures and forms throughout human history, causing individuals to do injustice

and inflict violence in ways that are sophisticated, planned and executed, and then accepted by society. And at the same time these mysteries of sorrow and suffering reveal how to remain, to abide in God and stay human in the presence of such evil. We try to imagine what Jesus went through in his pain, seeking to console and comfort God in our minds and hearts, and yet daily our God suffers in and through countless men, women, and children who suffer equally as terribly. Simone Weil once wrote about this love that we exhibit toward God; Jesus, incarnate and human among us, demands that we look at one another and ask this question: "Love of neighbor, in all its fullness, means asking him or her, 'What are you going through?' " And this question must be asked in regards to family members, those we work and study with, those we worship with and break our bread with, as well as those our government decides to wage war upon, invade and drop bombs upon or deny food, shelter, and medicine to in an exorbitant waste of resources on killing.

Jesus in this moment of sorrow has been beaten nearly unconscious and then he is made a fool of, draped in purple, a reed stuck in his hand and a crown fashioned of thick branches of a thornbush pushed into his scalp. He is spit on, taunted and mocked, insulted, his face slapped, and beaten. He is becoming unrecognizable as Jesus, as a human being. They are seeking to steal from him his personality, his dignity, and his sense of identity. He is laughed at, misunderstood, and derided. And there is no escape. After the soldiers tire of the game, he is dragged outside and held up on display, and the crowd, fast turning into a mob, is told to look at him.

This is our God incarnate. These are literally the words of Jesus coming back to us, saying: "Whatever you do to the least of your brothers and sisters, I take it you did it to me." (Matthew 25) This is our arrogance, disdain, and callous disregard for life standing before us and demanding that we look and see what we do to one another. This is the history of the human community and the history of sin incarnated in Jesus' body and blood. This is what power, authority, might, the world of nations and empires, the world of control and greed for more land and power looks like in the bodies of human beings caught in its grip. And this is Jesus laying down his life for his friends, for us, for all the earth, saying wordlessly that we are to treat one another with kindness, with regard, with tenderness and love, with respect and honor. And when we do not, then our souls and hearts become as rent and disfigured as what we do to one another in such hate. This is seeing God face-to-face and we are asked to comtemplate this face of God all around us. This is injustice and sin and we are told to contemplate this as well, to learn its contours and its consequences in the bodies of our brothers and sisters worldwide. This is the only king we will follow: the one who goes before us and into pain, suffering, and desolation, carrying us and our humanness in his heart and soul, showing us how to be human.

Did Jesus pray while he was struck? Did he mumble over and over again a cry for mercy to God? Did he blank out, with faces blurring indistinctly around him, sinking into pain that would not stop? How did he just hang on, continue to just stand up? What were his thoughts and feelings while he was beaten so that he could not be recognized for who he was? Jesus' suffering demands that we ask questions about what we think power is and how we are to use it, and what we think prayer is and what it is to be used for in our pain and weakness. The writer Wendell Berry in his novel *Jayber Crow* writes about this disturbing reality:

> For a while again I couldn't pray. I didn't dare to. In the most secret places of my soul I wanted to beg the Lord to reveal himself in power. I wanted to tell him that it was time for his coming. If there was anything at all to what he had promised, why didn't he come in glory with angels and lay his hands on the hurt children and awaken the dead soldiers and restore the burned villages and the blasted and poisoned land? Why didn't he cow our arrogance? . . .

This is Jesus' revelation of God, not in words, but in his body, his flesh and blood, his smashed and marred face, his blackened eyes and broken teeth, shivering in pain, exposed before hard-hearted people. And the only power on earth, the truest power on earth, is forgiveness, mercy, choosing not to react with violence or hate, absorbing the rage within and burying it in our own pain and bodies, stopping it forever. This is so strange, to us, this all-powerful love of our God. This is the power that we are called to as Jesus' friends and the children of God our Father. This is love that defers to all men and women as subjects of God's mercy and goodness. This is the kingdom of God, and the terrible risk to be human that our God has taken. And this Jesus, the Word made flesh, still chooses to dwell among us forever. This is the love of our God for us, for all that he has created. It is a mystery that is unfathomable, and yet one that we must immerse ourselves in continually so that we can learn the basic skills and arts of being human and made in the image and likeness of this God, Jesus, the suffering and Crucified One.

Let us pray. "Jesus, you are the king who serves. You are our king who is silent and who refuses to curse. You are our king who judges us justly and reveals to us what our sin does to others. You are our king who chooses to suffer with us rather than stop the suffering we do to one another. You mysteriously call us to suffer with others and to bear in our bodies our share of the burden of believing in your gospel. We are to remain in you and refuse to inflict pain on others, ever. We are to be known as those who dwell in your kingdom of mercy, of forgiveness and love, even of our enemies and of those who resist without violence no matter what harm is done unto us. This is the crown of courage and resistance, of being human in the face of evil that you mirror for us in your own sufferings and those of our brothers and sisters who are your brothers and sisters too. Jesus, crowned with thorns, never let us look upon the sufferings of others without moving toward them to embrace them, as we would your own body. Give us the courage to stand with you, witnesses to the truth of love, even to laying down our life, with you, for the transformation and conversion of the world. Amen."

THE FOURTH SORROWFUL MYSTERY:

The Way of the Cross

SCRIPTURES

From that moment Pilate tried to release him, but the Jews cried out, "If you release this man, you are no friend of Caesar. Anyone who makes himself king is defying Caesar."

When Pilate heard this, he had Jesus brought outside to the Stone Floor—in Hebrew *Gabbatha*—and there he had him seated in the tribune. It was the Preparation Day for the Passover, about noon. So Pilate said to the Jews, "Here is your king." But they cried out, "Away! Take him away! Crucify him!" Pilate replied, "Shall I crucify your king?" And the chief priests answered, "We have no king but Caesar."

Then Pilate handed Jesus over to them to be crucified. They took charge of him. Bearing his own cross, Jesus went out of the city to what is

called the Place of the Skull, in Hebrew:
Golgotha. There he was crucified and with him
two others, one on either side, and Jesus was in
the middle. (John 19:12–18)

Or,

The soldiers led him out of the city to crucify
him. On the way they met Simon of Cyrene, father of Alexander and Rufus, who was coming in
from the country, and forced him to carry the
cross of Jesus. When they had led him to the place
called Golgotha, which means the Skull, they offered him wine mixed with myrrh, but he would
not take it. Then they nailed him to the cross
and divided his clothes among themselves, casting
lots to decide what each should take. (Mark
15:20b–24, or Matthew 27:31–34)

Or,

When they led Jesus away, they seized Simon
of Cyrene, who was coming in from the fields,
and laid the cross on him, to carry it behind
Jesus.

A large crowd of people followed him; among
them were women beating their breast and wailing for him, but Jesus turned to them and said,
"Women of Jerusalem, do not weep for me, weep
rather for yourselves and for your children. For
the days are coming when people will say: 'Happy
are the women without child! Happy are those
who have not given birth or nursed a child!' And
they will say to the mountains: 'Fall on us!' And
to the hills: 'Cover us!' For if this is the lot of the

green wood, what will happen in the dry?" (Luke
23:26–31)

> *"He humbled himself by being obedient to death,
> death on the cross."*
>
> —PHILIPPIANS 2:8

Jesus is drawing near to the end of the way—his desti-
nation, the outskirts of Jerusalem, City of Peace. He
makes his torturous way through the streets, outside the
gate, and toward the hill called the Skull, the garbage
dump, where upright pieces of the cross are left standing
to instill into an oppressed people who their masters are,
and not let them forget it for even a moment. This is the
end of anyone who would dare to offer hope to people,
an alternative to the dominance of people by another nation. The way of the cross is all about power, about following, and about obedience.

Jesus preached to his disciples, and even to large
crowds, what following him would mean. He repeats again
and again the call to this way of the cross, but all who hear
this invitation to be his disciples resist his words. In
Mark's gospel he says:

> Then Jesus called the people and the disciples
> and said, "If you want to follow me, deny your-
> self, take up your cross and follow me. For if you
> choose to save your life, you will lose it; and if
> you lose your life for my sake and the sake of the
> Gospel, you will save it.

"What good is it to gain the whole world but destroy yourself? There is nothing you can give to recover your life. I tell you: if anyone is ashamed of me and of my words among this adulterous and sinful people, the Son of Man will also be ashamed of him when he comes in the Glory of his Father with the holy angels." (Mark 8:34–38)

This call to discipleship cuts to the heart of our lives. Who do we follow? Who do we obey? Who do we belong to? Where do our loyalties lie? And when we are up against the wall, so to speak, where do we stand? Do we belong to the kingdom of God first and foremost—the kingdom of justice and resistance to evil, but resistance that refuses to harm anyone else? Is our way the way of forgiveness seventy times seven, no matter what the sin? Do we look with favor on all the peoples of the world, as our God has looked with favor on us? In political as well as religious terms, by whose authority do we make our decisions and live? The way of the cross leads every follower eventually to this crux, this moment when we are tested and tried and either found wanting, or we find the cross laid upon our shoulders. In theological terms the question can be asked this way: Are we Christians who just happened to be born in the United States of America (or any other country), or are we Americans that just happened to get baptized?

In the short passage from the Gospel of John this question is strikingly clear. The people and their leaders are given a choice: Barabbas, a terrorist who had sought to overthrow the Romans violently, or Jesus, a prophet peacemaker who sought to bring people to a way of life in which all are treated with respect and dignity, and recognized as the children of God. The choice grows ugly. "Are you a friend of Caesar, the emperor (the president, the dictator, the prime minister, etc.)," or, "If you are a friend of this man, you are no friend of Caesar!" Choose! Choose death or choose life! This is the way of the cross, the way of Jesus, the way of life, the way of resistance without harm to others, and the way of peace on earth.

Philip Berrigan—a peacemaker in the tradition of his master, Jesus, who is Peace—who died in November 2002, wrote in a letter from prison in July 2000 these words about the way of the cross.

> This much is clear: discipleship is the way of the cross. And the cross has a distinct meaning for us. It means punishment by the State for dissent, especially civil resistance, wherein man's unjust law is broken to keep God's law. It meant execution for Jesus, as it often does in the Third World. It often means torture and punishment there. In the United States, Canada, Western Europe it means imprisonment. That is what modern Christians fear—the cross. It is also what the disciples feared: they knew what the Romans did to zealots and troublemakers. Their crosses and their victims dotted the landscape. That is why I ask my fellow seekers, "Can you—can any-

one serious about following Jesus today—remain safe and secure and legal?" (From "The Plough Reader," The Bruderhof Foundation, on-line at http://www.bruderhof.com)

To us this may seem extreme, but this was the experience of every disciple for more than the first three hundred and fifty or more years of the early Church. To be baptized automatically put one in jeopardy of one's livelihood and life, in opposition to the authority of Rome. And throughout history, each group of Christians in every country has known persecution and martyrdom—the way of the cross—for truly being Christian and following the way of Jesus instead of the way of the culture, the way of the country, the way of the government and nation. Today, to be a disciple demands that we stand against any government that legalizes abortion, euthanasia, the death penalty, the use of nuclear weapons or the creation of new nuclear weapons, or uses the tactics of unprovoked aggressive attacks on countries that have not attacked us, torture, detainment of persons without due cause, and disregard for the rights of all people.

In this third millennium, just a few years old, we are being summoned to discern whether or not war can ever be an option among peoples, because of the way wars are fought, with massive civilian casualties: in the 1900s, more than 90 percent of the casualties of war were soldiers, and by the end of the century, more than 90 percent of the casualties were civilians. Thomas Merton wrote in the mid-sixties this trenchant line: "The God of peace is never served or worshipped by violence." John Paul II has been the first to say that "war is not an option" any longer in our world, that it is a "crime against peace and a tragedy for all religious people." On Good Friday, 2003, the Pope's preacher, Father Raniero Cantala- messa, chose as his theme the peace of Christ. In the col- umn "The Church in the World" in *The Tablet,* April 26, 2003, the emphasis on the celebration of the Stations of the Cross was reported.

> (He) chose as his theme the peace of Christ, comparing the Gospel message with attempts throughout history to impose peace through war. He contrasted the Pax Romana of the Emperor Augustus at the time of Christ with "another, su- perior kind" of peace brought by Jesus. Today, he said, "the world order demands that Christ's way to peace replace Augustus." The only way to peace is by "destroying enmity, not the enemy," the Capuchin friar added. He then quoted Abraham Lincoln: "Do I not destroy my enemies when I make them my friends?" (He added) "Millions of people with no peace in their hearts, or of families without peace in their homes, will never make a humankind at peace." (p. 26)

During the Last Supper, Jesus was clear to give his friends and disciples a gift to accompany us as we follow him on his way of the cross—the gift of peace. He cries out to them: "Peace by with you: I give you my peace. Not as the world gives peace do I give it to you. Do not be troubled; do not be afraid." (John 14:27) these are the first words of the Risen Lord to his friends, still locked in fear: "Peace be with you!" (John 20:19) The one we follow even unto death, is the peace of God with us, and among us.

But this way of the cross begins and is practiced personally, in our families and churches, workplaces and schools. It begins with forgiveness, with speaking the truth and standing up for what you believe in, and in refusing to do what others expect us to do, because everyone else is doing it. It begins with compassion, with the corporal and spiritual works of mercy, with sharing our resources and encouraging one another. It is part and parcel of every minute of our lives, in all our relationships, decisions, and situations. It begins and ends with love: love of our neighbor and loving others as we would have them love and treat us. And it is love of our enemies, in obedience to the command of Jesus to pray for them, do good to them, and not to harm them. And it matures into obedience to the command to his friends the night he is handed over to the violence of the state and local community: "Love one another as I have loved you." This is the way of the cross, the way of Jesus, the way we are to live in the world if we call ourselves disciples of Jesus. The writer Evelyn Underhill, more than half a century ago, wrote what this might mean:

To look at the crucifix and then to look at our own hearts is to test by the cross the quality of our love—if we do that honestly and unflinchingly we don't need any other self-examination. The lash, the crown of thorns, the mockery, the stripping, the nails—life has equivalents of all these for us and God asks a love for himself and his children which can accept and survive all that in the particular way in which it is offered to us. It is no use to talk in a large vague way about the love of God; here is its point of insertion in the world. ("Bread and Wine: Readings for Lent and Easter," The Bruderhof Foundation, on-line at http://www.bruderhof.com)

From the moment of our baptisms, when we promise to live "in the freedom of the children of God" upon the earth and to "resist evil and refuse to be mastered by sin" and to "live under no sign of power but the sign of the cross," we begin following in the footsteps of Jesus, walking the way of the cross—all the way to Golgotha and to our small moments of crucifixion. We do not walk alone. We follow behind Jesus. And as we hear in the story of Simon of Cyrene carrying the cross of Jesus and following behind him, we often have others to lift our burden and fall in behind us. We too are exhorted to bear our share of the burden of the gospel, to fill up what is lacking in the sufferings of Christ, and to pick up the cross of those we meet long the way. As Jesus warned the women who stood along his way and wept, not to weep for him, but for themselves and their children, we must weep for all the people of the world who will know horror and death by violence. The way of the cross is repeated in millions of places and in the lives of people worldwide. We are not to stand weeping, but to reach out and lift the burden placed on others' shoulders and to fall in behind them, walking the way together with our crucified Lord.

Let us pray. "Jesus, you are scorned and rejected by the mob, your own people, and even your disciples, whom you call your friends, and you are led out to be crucified. The cross is laid on you. You begin the walk that will end in your death, hanging nailed to the wood that you bear now on your shoulders. This is the burden of the truth you have spoken and the Truth you are as the Word of God made flesh in our world. This is the burden of forgiveness and peace that you bring to every human being as the gift of compassion from our Father. Let us walk behind you, bearing our burden of the gospel, the cross that is laid upon us for speaking the truth and standing up for your Word in our world. Let us keep you always in our sight, remembering that you have shared our pain and sufferings and have gone before us so that we might carry our cross and die with trust in God's ultimate justice and judgment. Jesus, do not let us ever lay the cross on others by our sin, our evil, our injustice, or our participation in the violence and wars of the world. Let us remember this every time we sign ourselves with the cross: In the name of the Father and of the Son and of the Holy Spirit. Amen."

THE FIFTH SORROWFUL MYSTERY:

The Crucifixion and Death of Jesus

SCRIPTURE

There at the place called The Skull, he was crucified together with the criminals—one on his right
and another on his left. Jesus said, "Father, forgive them for they do not know what they do."
And the guards cast lots to divide his clothes
among themselves.

The people stood by watching. As for the
rulers, they jeered at him, saying to one another,
"Let the man who saved others now save himself,
for he is the Messiah, the chosen one of God!"

. . . One of the criminals hanging with Jesus
insulted him, "So you are the Messiah? Save
yourself and us as well!" But the other rebuked
him, saying, "Have you no fear of God, you who
received the same sentence as he did? For us it is
just: this is payment for what we have done. But
this man has done nothing wrong." And he said,
"Jesus, remember me when you come into your
kingdom." Jesus replied, "Truly, you will be with
me today in paradise."

It was now about noon. The sun was hidden
and darkness came over the whole land until
mid-afternoon, and at that time the curtain of
the Sanctuary was torn in two. Then Jesus gave a

loud cry, "Father, into your hands I commend my spirit." And saying that, he gave up his spirit. (Luke 23:33–35, 39–46)

Or,

With that Jesus knew all was now finished and he said, I am thirsty, to fulfil what was written in scripture. A jar full of bitter wine stood there; so, putting a sponge soaked in the wine on a twig of hyssop, they raised it to his lips. Jesus took the wine and said, "It is accomplished." Then he bowed his head and gave up the spirit. (John 19:25–30)

Or,

When noon came, darkness fell over the whole land and lasted until three o'clock; and at three o'clock Jesus cried out in a loud voice, "Eloi, Eloi, lama sabachthani?" which means "My God, my God, why have you deserted me?" As soon as they heard these words, some of the bystanders said, "Listen! He is calling for Elijah." And one of them went quickly to fill a sponge with bitter wine and, putting it on a reed, gave him to drink saying, "Now let's see whether Elijah comes to take him down."

But Jesus uttered a loud cry and gave up his spirit. (Mark 15:33–37 and Matthew 27:45–50)

> *Teach us to give voice to new life in the world because you dry the tears of the oppressed and death shall be no more.*

—LUIS ESPINAL, SJ

This moment, the death of Jesus by crucifixion, is somehow the center of all life, the turning point of all history, the meaning and the threshold of what it means to be human and to be holy. This is the death of God in the flesh, the heart and soul of Jesus. Jesus is human and goes to his death refusing to resist it, which is exacted of him by human beings who, from the beginning, have killed and refused to live. The first sin, in the book of Genesis, is fratricide: the killing of Abel by his brother, Cain. And yet, even then, God will not allow anyone to kill Cain in retaliation or vengeance. He is marked out as a wanderer and a fugitive on the earth, but God declares that if anyone kills Cain, the murderer will suffer vengeance seven times for what he does. (Genesis 4:8–15) But somehow, this murder of Jesus by human beings will reverse the order of creation that has been bent from the beginning. Now the arc of the world will bend toward forgiveness, reconciliation, and life.

This dying alters all of life. And from this moment forth, all our lives are rooted in the cross and in the body of the Crucified One, crying out and handing over his life, his Spirit, to the Father. In the life and death of Jesus we find that our mortal lives are what matter most to our God. We must stand and look at our God, Jesus nailed up on the tree and dying. This is the mystery of our God come to us, dwelling with us, and even dying with us and for us so that we might know what life is and how we are to live, and so to die, as human beings, the beloved children of God. This moment of death says so much about our God. John Stott wrote:

I could never myself believe in God, if it were not for the cross. The only God I believe in is the one Nietzsche ridiculed as "God on the Cross." In the real world of pain, how could one worship a God who was immune to it? I have entered many Buddhist temples and stood respectfully before the statute of Buddha, his legs crossed, arms folded, eyes closed, the ghost of a smile playing round his mouth, a remote look on his face, detached from the agonies of the world. But each time after a while I have to turn away. And in imagination I have turned instead to that lonely, twisted, tortured figure on the cross, nails through hands and feet, back lacerated, limbs wrenched, brow bleeding from thorn-pricks, mouth dry and intolerably thirsty, plunged into God-forsaken darkness. That is the God for me! He laid aside his immunity to pain. He entered our world of flesh and blood, tears and death. He suffered for us. ("Bread and Wine: Readings for Lent and Easter," The Bruderhof Foundation, on-line at http//www.bruderhof.com)

Perhaps even more to the point, he suffered with us as a human being, and in that suffering and dying he demands that we choose: Are we those who live or those who practice death? Are we those who do justice or those who unjustly, though perhaps legally, kill? Are we those who nurture and protect life or are we among those who destroy and wreak vengeance on the living? Are we those who seek what is good or are we those who do evil and put others there—on the cross? Or as Brenden Lovett wrote in *It's Not Over Yet!* this is what the memory and contemplation of the passion of Jesus means for the world: "The *memoria passionis* will always be that which generates creative action for life. . . . The challenge will only be met by people who are keeping alive the memory and awareness of past and present suffering and whose lives and thinking revolve now about practical concern for victims, a concern that ensures that the evil will not keep happening." (p. 42, op. cit.)

This is life lived with love, unto death, even death on a cross. This is the love of our God for all human beings. This is what it is meant to be: the fullness of life in the face of evil, sin, injustice, and death. This is the final statement of the life of Jesus: even death cannot kill love. Even life is stronger than hate and violent death. Somehow in looking on the Crucified One we can find the power of life and the power of love that Jesus lived by and through and in: God our Father. Our God looks like this: human beings loving in the face of death, and so truly living as human beings made in the image of God. Our God dies so that we might have ever more life! And so we must die in order to live; die every day, die small deaths so that there is ever more life. This is the power and paradoxically the powerlessness of our God in Jesus.

Jon Sobrino, SJ, one of the Jesuits that the Salvadorean military intended to kill when they broke into the University of El Salvador several decades ago, once said that there are only two kinds of people in the world: those who crucify and those who uncrucify. As we stand at the foot of the cross, listening to the words of Jesus offering forgiveness to the one who sides with him as he dies, we must decide whether we live and die by this act of forgiving or whether we align ourselves with those who jeer and taunt and curse the suffering servant Jesus. We listen to Jesus cry out the words of Psalm 22: "My God, my God, why have you forsaken me? Why are you so far from me, from the sound of my groaning?"

What follows are twenty lines of agony, of pain torn from the body of a human being reduced to "a worm and not human" by other human beings that are more like "vicious dogs" in their attacking of him. Yet the closing words of the psalm must make us stop and listen even more carefully because they are the prayer of a human being who believes and trusts, even as he is brutally and viciously destroyed. He is more human than any other person there. We hear the first words of the psalm prayed aloud in the mouth of Jesus. But these were the words he would have prayed silently before handing over his spirit to the heart of God, his Father.

> *I will proclaim your name to my brothers.*
> *I will praise you in the assembly.*
> *All you who fear the Lord, praise him!*
> *All you sons of Jacob, glorify him!*
> *All you sons of Israel, revere him!*

> *For he has not scorned or loathed the afflicted in his misery.*
> *He has not hidden his face from me but has listened when I cried to him.*

I will praise you in the great assembly,
fulfil my vows before all who revere you.
The lowly will eat and be satisfied.
Those who seek the Lord will praise him.
May your hearts live forever!

The whole earth from end to end will acknowledge and turn to the
    Lord;
the families of nations will worship him.
For dominion belongs to the Lord and he reigns over the nations.
Before him all those who rest in the earth will bow down,
all who go down in the dust.

My soul will live for him. My descendants will serve him
and proclaim the Lord to coming generations;
they will announce his salvation to a people yet unborn.
These are the things that he has done. (Psalm 22:23–32)

This is the prayer of Jesus on the cross. And then
Jesus cries out again and hands over his life, his heart,
and his spirit to God. This is his last prayer. This is his
last cry of life. This is his cry against death, against violence, against evil, against sin. This is the cry of all victims: the cry of all those murdered, the cry of all the
oppressed, the cry of all those who have suffered at the
hands of others. This is the cry for justice and the cry for
God's presence to be found in every moment of life, especially in the last moment, when life is torn from us.
Jesus gives that last cry, that last breath, that last love,

gathering his whole life into the safekeeping of God. It is his last testimony: to life and to the God of life, the Father he so loves, and to our lives.

Even in this last moment of Godforsakenness there is forgiveness and life. There is prayer and trust. There is belief and the demand to be known. This is Jesus the Crucified One, human and divine. This is what we are to stand and contemplate and become: human, holy, graced, and alive, even as we die—handing over our lives and our bodies in death as an act of worship to the God of the living. Even as Jesus cries out in distress, he is seeking the God of light. To be human is to be always seeking God, to be reaching for the God of life. This is the truth of Jesus and now there is nothing on the face of the earth, no extremity of suffering that is not found in our God, taken and held and transformed. In every moment of suffering and death we can find our God, who has borne our humanity and known our mortality in his crucifixion and death. We are saved now, even from the hold, the terror, and the threat of death.

Our God despises and abhors suffering, especially that we inflict upon one another, but he will not allow it to be the last word. The last word is love! Love in spite of hate and violence. Love in spite of mercilessness and brutality. Love in spite of the refusal to forgive and the refusal to live as human beings. Love in spite of sin and death. Love in spite of the silence of God. Love in spite of sensing being separate from God. Love in spite of the worst that people can do. Just love with justice, with mercy, and with peace. But we must stand there and watch Jesus die. Watch as he cries out and hands over his spirit to the Father. Watch and see what we are capable of when we refuse to love, and refuse to live, and refuse to cling to the God of life.

Let us pray. "Jesus, we stand before your cross. We stand before your bleeding and tortured body that hangs as witness to our evil and sin. We stand before your presence mangled and emptied out in mercy and love. We stand and hear your prayer, your trust in God, and your command for us to worship God alone. We stand and try to pray with you. We stand and with you, hand over our lives into the heart of God. May we live and die remembering and aware of your love and faithfulness. May we obey our Father of life with you, by the power of your Spirit, and never succumb to the evil of sin, violence, and death. We ask this through your Spirit given over to God and to your church and into our hearts. Amen."

The Glorious Mysteries
of the Rosary

SIX

John Paul introduces the glorious mysteries with ringing words of hope:

"The contemplation of Christ's face cannot stop at the image of the Crucified One. He is the Risen One!" [JPII, Apostolic Letter *Novo Millennio Ineunte* (January 6, 2001), 28:AAS 93 (2001), 284.] The Rosary has always expressed this knowledge born of faith and has invited the believer to pass beyond the darkness of the passion in order to gaze upon Christ's glory in the resurrection and ascension. Contemplating the Risen One,

Christians rediscover the reasons for their own faith (cf. 1 Corinthians 15:14) and relive the joy not only of those to whom Christ appeared—the Apostles, Mary Magdalene and the disciples on the road to Emmaus—but also the joy of Mary, who must have had an equally intense experience of the new life of her glorified Son. (RVM, #23)

The glorious mysteries look at the Risen Christ in glory, after his leaving earth to sit at the right hand of his Father, where he prays and intercedes for us until the fullness of time. Then the mysteries look at the birth of the Church at Pentecost with the sending of the Spirit upon those who waited in joy and prayer to "be clothed from on high with the power of God" that would enable them to go out into the world and make disciples of all peoples, obeying Jesus' command. Traditionally this is where the glorious mysteries stopped speaking of Jesus and switched over to Mary. In keeping with the exhortation to reflect upon the mysteries of Jesus' life on earth and in glory, two more glorious mysteries will be presented here for reflection. The fourth glorious mystery will be that of the Coming of the Son of Man in Glory to Judge the Nations and the fifth and final mystery of the Rosary will be that of the mystery of the Trinity, the fullness of the revelation of the Scriptures, and the fullness of life in God that each of us is initiated into in our baptisms, and encouraged to continue in, in faithfulness as we fulfill our lives as believers, and to share in that glory forever. Hopefully these glorious mysteries will fill out the beliefs and hopes of Christians more scripturally and substantially than the ones dedicated to traditional beliefs about Mary after her death. Revelation does not end with the feast of Pentecost, and the Church's faith in Jesus continues through history and far into the future with the hope of judgment and justice and communion and life in the Trinity as the end of all our prayers and faithfulness.

THE FIRST GLORIOUS MYSTERY:

The Raising of Jesus from the Dead

SCRIPTURE

When the Sabbath was over, Mary of Magdala, Mary the mother of James and Salome brought spices so that they might go and anoint the body. And very early in the morning on the first day of the week, just after sunrise, they came to the tomb. They were saying to one another, "Who will roll back the stone from the entrance to the tomb?" But as they looked up, they noticed that the stone had already been rolled away. It was a huge one.

As they entered the tomb, they saw a young man in a white robe seated on the right, and they were amazed. But he said to them, "Don't be afraid. I know that you are seeking Jesus of Nazareth the Crucified One. He has been raised. He is not here. This is, however, the place where they laid him. Now go and tell his disciples, and Peter: he is going ahead of you to Galilee; you will see him there just as he told you." The women ran out from the tomb and fled, for terror and amazement had seized them. And they were so afraid that they said nothing to anyone. (Mark 16:1–8)

Or,

They immediately set out and returned to Jerusalem. There they found the Eleven and their companions gathered together. They were greeted by these words: "Yes, it is true, the Lord is risen! He has appeared to Simon!" then the two told what had happened on the road and how Jesus made himself known when he broke bread with them.

As they went on talking about this, Jesus himself stood in their midst. And he said to them, "Peace to you." In their panic and fright they thought that they were seeing a ghost, but he said to them, "Why are you upset and why do such ideas cross your mind? Look at my hands and feet and see that it is I myself. Touch me and see for yourselves that a ghost has not flesh and bones as I have." As he said this, he showed them his hands and feet.

. . . Then Jesus said to them, "Remember the words I spoke to you when I was still with you:

Everything written about me in the Law of Moses, the Prophets and the Psalms had to be fulfilled." Then he opened their minds to understand the Scriptures. (Luke 24:33–45)

Or, Luke 24:1–12, the story of the women in the morning at the tomb, or Luke 24:13–35, the story of Emmaus, or Matthew 28, the resurrection and the meeting of Jesus on the way, or John 20:19–29, Jesus' appearance to the disciples in the locked room, on the evening of the resurrection.

> *Christ has conquered! Glory fills you! Darkness*
> *vanishes forever!*
> *Christ is the Morning Star, who came back from*
> *the dead,*
> *and shed his peaceful light on all humankind.*

—THE EXSULTET

This mystery is the core of our religion. We read all the Scriptures backward from this moment. It is the Resurrection of Jesus that gives meaning to all that has gone before and opens to us the depth of what he said and how he lived. God the Father lovingly raised Jesus from the dead in the power of the Spirit. That is the foundational statement and bedrock of our belief. Without it there is nothing to stake our life on and nothing to keep us from fearing death. We believe that what the Father has done for Jesus in the power of the Spirit, the Father will one day do for us—raise us from the dead in the power of the Spirit. And even more, we believe that this experience of resurrection—of death being stronger and surer than life, of justice and mercy being truer than evil and hate, of love overriding all else in the world—for us begins in our baptisms. When we are buried with Christ and come forth from the waters into the life of faith, we are told, "You live now, no longer for yourselves alone, but now you live hidden with Christ in God."

This night turned into glorious day, this dawn of the new creation, this shift in all of history toward redemption and hope, is so filled with joy that it is hard to speak about. The ancient writer Hippolytus of Rome sang out:

> *Christ is risen! The world below lies desolate.*
> *Christ is risen! The spirits of evil are fallen.*
> *Christ is risen! The angels of God rejoice.*
> *Christ is risen! The tombs of the dead are empty.*
> *Christ is risen indeed from the dead—*
> *The first of the sleepers. And glory and power are his forever and*
> *ever. Amen.*

This is the night to sing the Exsultet, which rises and rises to a pitch of intensity and awe that almost shatters us with joy. These words just begin to speak of what is happening in the world that will change all of history forever. "The power of this holy night dispels all evil, washes guilt away, restores lost innocence, brings mourners joy; it casts out hatred, brings us peace, and humbles earthly pride." This is the day to sing the Gloria as an exultant hymn to the work of God in Jesus and the loosing of Jesus' own Spirit from death. This is a day to sing the Magnificat originally found in Mary's mouth before her child was born. Mary's song echoes or is prelude to the Exsultet that praises the Paschal Candle, the light of Christ now raised high before us, as the cross was raised just days earlier.

Words and images stumble and stutter seeking to express the impossible, what must be believed before it can be understood or even proclaimed in song and life. But this is the night and morning that ushers in new creation and reveals what God has done and is doing for those he has created in his image and loves, loves even unto death and resurrection. This is Mary's song of praise and exualtation found in Luke 1:46–55, rewritten for the celebration of both the Incarnation and the Resurrection of Jesus, the Beloved Child of God, Word made flesh among us. It is the prayer that fills all our mouths and souls with wild joy and unbelievable gratitude for the sheer goodness of our God.

> *My soul proclaims the greatness of the Lord,*
> *my spirit exalts in God my savior!*
> *God has looked upon all his servants in their lowliness and people*
> *will cry throughout the earth the blessings of the Father who has*
> *stooped to breathe upon his beloved Son and has raised him*
> *from the dead.*
>
> *The Holy and Mighty One has done unbelieveable things for us,*
> *Holy is his Name: we cry out with the angels and all creation:*

Holy! Holy! Holy! And blessed is he who comes in the name of the Lord: Jesus the Crucified now raised up from the dead!

From age to age his mercy extends to those who dwell in his presence.
And now his mercy breaks the hold of even death so that our lives are filled with tenderness and hope for life everlasting, even here on earth.
He has acted with power and done wonders.
He has sent his Beloved Son as Word made flesh, made human among us! His child spoke truth, touched all flesh with passionate devotion and lifted those bowed down in despair and sin. This Jesus saved us and stood against evil and violence resisting all evil and hatred. He took it into his own body dying in horror yet dying humanly, forgiving and trusting and loving to the end.
Now has God scattered the proud in their conceit and shattered all their plans. Those who destroyed in might and war are taken down from their high places and those who were trodden underfoot, bruised and ignored are now lifted up with care.
All those who hungered for food and justice, for a life worth living and hope now sing good tidings and bless one another in peace while those who were rich, greedy and hoarded their resources find themselves as empty-handed as their hearts.

Our Father held out his hand to Israel, his servant, and was always remembering us with mercy. Now his hand is stretched out to all the peoples of the earth, even as he promised our ancestors so long ago.
Our God has shattered death and lives forever.

Now we, the beloved children of God, stand with Jesus who is
crucified and risen from the dead and we cry out our joy.
Now we live forever in the freedom of the children of God.
Now we are the peacemakers who walk hand in hand with our
hearts bound together in the Spirit of Jesus the Crucified One
who lives forever and dwells with us forever.
Give glory to the Father, the Son and the Spirit with all your body
and soul. Amen Amen Alleluia.

What is resurrection life? We believe in the resurrection of Jesus, that the Father raised him up and he lives forever. We believe that our Father will raise us from the dead and that we will live forever because of the life, death, and resurrection of Jesus, who has reconciled us to God and bound us to one another in his peace, his very body, and his presence. We believe that we are baptized into Jesus' resurrection and our new life in the Spirit, with the privilege and power to call God our Father. With Jesus begins our being sealed in the Spirit and baptized in the waters of joy and life. Our lives, as believers and as Christians, are practice for the resurrection we will know after our deaths. Resurrection is more about life than about death. Because of Jesus being raised from the dead, we do not have to fear death. We believe that we have died with Christ and so we will live with him and one day know his glory as our own. All of this is our heritage and our gift because of the great love of our God in sending Jesus his Beloved Child to become human with us, living and dying and rising with us. The pastor Dietrich Bonhoeffer wrote these words: "We pay more attention to dying than to death. We're more concerned to get over the act of dying than to overcome death. Socrates mastered the art of dying; Christ overcame death as the last enemy. There is a real difference between the two things; the one is within the scope of human possibilities, the other means resurrection." (From *Letters & Papers from Prison,* Dietrich Bonhoeffer, Touchstone Books, 1997)

Christ has conquered death! We are not bound or in thrall to death. We are bound to the life of Christ, who never dies. The empty tomb is the first symbol in all the resurrection accounts of the gospels. There is no body there, the body of Christ is now alive in the community. The body of Christ is now present in the Eucharist, in the Word of the Scriptures, in the presence of the poor among us, and in the Church. The Acts of the Apostles is read first during the Easter season because this is the new body of Christ in the world. This community of believers in the Risen Lord hold all things in common and care for each other with the reverence and respect they would care for the body of Christ, the person of Jesus. The Didache, an early Church document from the second century, describes much of the liturgical and daily life of the Church: "See how those Christians love one another, there are no poor among them." This is a new reality, a new body, a new community where there are "no rich, no poor, no slave, no free, no man, no woman, no Jew, no Gentile," because all of these disparate groups are one, bound together in faith and obedience to Jesus the Risen

Lord. This community grew and matured under persecution and martyrdom and by being "faithful to the teaching of the apostles, the common life of sharing and the breaking of the bread and the prayers." (Acts 2:42) This marvelous reality was based on the resurrection of Jesus. In the words of Peter's sermon,

> God raised him to life and released him from the pain of death, because it was impossible for him to be held in the power of death. David spoke of him when he said: I saw the Lord before me at all times; he is by my side, that I may not be shaken. Therefore my heart was glad and my tongue rejoiced; my body too will live in hope. Because you will not forsake me in the abode of the dead, nor allow your Holy One to experience corruption. You have made known to me the paths of life, and your presence will fill me with joy. (Acts 2:24–28)

This is our belief. This is what we stake our lives on. This is our hope and our steadfast foundation. This is all done by the goodness of our God. This is why we are Christians. This is how we live. We live in the body of Christ risen from the dead. In the ancient baptismal words: "We live, now, no longer for ourselves alone, but now we live hidden with Christ in God."

Let us pray. "Lord, this night we carve the date, this year into the Paschal Candle, for this year will belong to you and our lives will belong to you alone. We inscribe the candle with these words: 'All times belong to him and all the ages.' Then we mark the candle with the four red marks of your cross, praying: 'By your holy and glorious wounds may you, O Christ our Lord, guard us and keep us.' And as the candle is lit with the holy fire we proclaim: 'May the light of Christ, rising in glory, dispel the darkness of our hearts and minds.' O Jesus Christ, you are risen from the dead and now death is not the last word. Your word to us always now is love. Your word is life. Your word is hope. And your word is 'I am the Resurrection and the Life, if you believe in me you will never die; and if you die I will bring you to life again!' Lord, we do believe! Amen, Alleluia, Alleluia, Amen."

THE SECOND GLORIOUS MYSTERY:

The Ascension of Jesus

SCRIPTURE

And he went on, "You see what was written: the Messiah had to suffer and on the third day rise from the dead. Then repentance and forgiveness in his name would be proclaimed to all the nations, beginning from Jerusalem. Now you shall be witnesses to this. And this is why I will send you what my Father promised. So remain in the city until you are clothed with power from above."

Jesus led them almost as far as Bethany; then he lifted up his hands and blessed them. And as he blessed them, he withdrew (and was taken to heaven. They worshiped him). They returned to Jerusalem full of joy and were continually in the Temple praising God. (Luke 24:45b–53)

Or,

". . . you will receive power when the Holy Spirit comes upon you; and you will be my witnesses in Jerusalem, throughout Judea and Samaria, even to the ends of the earth."

After Jesus said this, he was taken up before their eyes and a cloud hid him from their sight. While they were still looking up to heaven where he went, suddenly, two men dressed in white stood beside them, and said, "Men of Galilee, why do you stand here looking up at the sky? This Jesus who has been taken from you into heaven will return in the same way as you have seen him go there." (Acts 1:8–11)

> *May we follow him into the new creation, for his ascension is our glory and our hope.*

> —FROM "ASCENSION OF
> THE LORD," COLLECT

This mystery is a bridge or a link between the events of the Resurrection of the Lord on Easter morning and the sending of the gift of the Spirit on Pentecost. It is a mystery about time, about endurance and waiting, and about hope. It is about looking and seeing in such a way that what has been seen is integrated and absorbed with faith, the inner eye. Jesus' disciples and friends have seen so much that they need time and prayer to come to understand what has transpired and to deal with the startling new knowledge of who Jesus actually is instead of their individual perceptions of him. Liturgically, the Easter season lasts for seven weeks, with the Feast of the Ascension coming ten days before Pentecost. In the gospel accounts, especially in Luke, Matthew, and John, the momentous experiences of the Resurrection, the Ascension, and the gifting of the Spirit happen all at once: the evening of Easter Sunday night. But this is too much for the human mind and spirit to comprehend all at once. There is the essential need to reflect upon, distill, and look with prayer intently in remembrance of all these things before moving on or attempting to put into practice what Jesus has commanded them to do.

He has conferred on them the responsibility and privilege of being his witnesses in the world, beginning here in their own place, in Jerusalem, and then moving out to those around them, in Judea and Samaria (home to enemies of the Jews), and then out into all of the new creation. *Witness* first means to see—really see, so that it becomes part and parcel of one's being. Mark Doty, an essayist, writes in *Still Life* what this seeing entails. He is speaking about looking at a painting but his words can easily apply to looking at a piece of scripture, the remembered words of Jesus, an experience and the presence of the Spirit in prayer: "I have felt the energy and life of the painting's will; I have been held there, instructed. And the overall effect, the result of looking and looking into its brimming surface as long as I could look, is love, by which I mean a sense of tenderness toward experience, of being held within an intimacy with the things of this world."

The disciples need time to see this way, learning intimacy with remembrance and adding depth to their perceptions so that even details and repetitive phrases of Jesus become familiar and known in body, mind, and soul. The mystery of the Resurrection takes a lifetime of concentration and contemplation just to find a language to speak of it, let alone come to live out of its power and meaning. Saint Leo the Great, pope from 440 to 461 A.D., wrote of this feast in one of his homilies.

> Through all this time, dearly beloved, which went by between the resurrection of the Lord and his ascension, the providence of God took thought for this, taught this, and penetrated their eyes and heart with this: that they should recognize the Lord Jesus Christ as truly risen, who was truly born, truly suffered, and truly died. The blessed apostles and all the disciples who had been frightened by his death on the cross and were doubtful with respect to faith in his resurrection were strengthened by the manifest truth. The result was that not only were they not affected with sadness but were filled with "great joy" when the Lord went into the heights of heaven.

Ascension is a hard mystery in a sense that the disciples saw the Risen Lord and then his bodily physical presence was taken from them. The words "taken from them" have a ring of loss, of interruption, and yet of accomplishment. It is a turning point in their lives and faith. Resurrection, the shattering of all the laws of existence, of life and death, is a shock to their minds: after the tantalizing presence of the Risen Lord, he is again gone from their sight. This mystery invites us to stand on the threshold of the reality of Jesus now sitting at the right hand of the Father in heaven, pleading and interceding on our behalf yet, still with us, as he promised, until the end of time.

This mystery introduces us to the amazing concept that now, until forever, until the coming of Christ in glory, Jesus, the Crucified and Risen One, prays for us, with us, and in us. This mystery of Jesus' presence both among us in communion and in God the Father by the power of the Spirit changes forever how we pray. In John's gospel, Jesus has tried to warn and comfort us:

A little while and you will see me no more, and then a little while, and you will see me."

Some of the disciples wondered, "What does he mean by: 'A little while and you will not see me, and then a little while and you will see me'? And why did he say: 'I go to the Father'? And they said to one another, "What does he mean by 'a little while'? We don't understand."

Jesus said to them "You feel sorrowful now,

but I will see you again, and your hearts will rejoice. And no one will take your joy from you.
When that day comes you will not ask me anything. Truly, I say to you, whatever you ask the
Father in my Name, he will give you. So far you
have not asked in my Name, ask and receive that
your joy may be full.

"I taught you all this in veiled language, but
the time is coming when I shall no longer speak
in veiled language, but will tell you plainly of the
Father.

"When that day comes, you will ask in my
Name and it will not be for me to ask the Father
for you, for the Father himself loves you because
you have loved me and you believe that I came
from the Father. As I came from the Father and
have come into the world, so I am leaving the
world and going to the Father." (John 16:16–19,
22–28)

Immediately after these words of Jesus, the disciples are
relieved and believe that now they understand Jesus
clearly and yet, as Jesus listens to them declare their faith
in him, he responds by telling them that before the night
is through they will all either betray him or run from
him, leaving him to face the cross alone—but in his
words: "Yet I am not alone, for the Father is with me. I
have told you all this, so that in me you may have peace.
You will have trouble in the world; but courage! I have
overcome the world." (John 16: 32b–33) This is the necessary time that we all need to come to deeper belief, and

to learn to listen underneath to the words of Jesus, conscious that we do not know and we do not understand practically anything!

One of the evening prayers for this feast speaks of our hope: "You came down from heaven on a pilgrimage of love, grant that we may take the same path to your presence." And yet, we know his presence now in the Scriptures, the Eucharist, the community of believers, and in all the world, especially among the poor and those who struggle for the truth, for justice and peace. This time between Easter and Pentecost, between the eastering moments of our lives and the coming of the Spirit with insight and understanding, is the time for learning to live with grace, with paradox, and with hope.

We must let the mysteries of God's love for us seep deep into our souls and penetrate our minds and lives so that we come to believe in God's plan for creation and history. Jesus born among us, living with us, dying and rising, is still among us, and the yet-to-be-fulfilled triumph of the hopes of God are now set in motion and will inevitably come to completion. Redemptive grace is now a factor that must be reckoned into every decision and experience of history. And the presence of the Risen Jesus, who has ascended to "my Father and to your Father, to my God, who is your God" (John 20:17b), gives us access to God in an entirely new way. The power of God in Jesus is now shared with us, his friends and followers, and we pray with Jesus for that power to be released continually upon the earth in how we witness to God in our words, decisions, and lives, lived as an alternative to what the kingdoms of this world claim as life.

There is an old Latin hymn called "Aterne Rex" (translated by Thomas Aquinas Byrnes, OP) that sings of our belief, our hope, and our praise of what God has done for us in Jesus, and what God will continue to do in us until the fullness of time.

> *Ascending to the throne at the right hand of the Father,*
> *All power is given to Jesus from heaven, which power was not given*
> *by men. So that the threefold fabric of the universe—the*
> *creatures of heaven, earth and hell—may now bend the knee*
> *in subjection.*
> *Be thou our joy who are to be our reward; let our glory ever be in*
> *thee through all the ages. O Lord, ascending above the stars, to*
> *thee be glory, together with the Father, and the Holy Spirit for*
> *ever.*

Let us pray. "Jesus, you are taken up into glory and taken from our sight and yet you exhort us to be joyful and to wait for still another gift from our Father. Now, throughout all of time, our own times and all of history, you are seated at the right hand of the Father and you pray for us and with us as we seek to be your witnesses in the world and continue your transformation of the world. May we always obey you, as believers and as your Church, living and praying in hope together. May we remember that as your living witnesses we must restore joy to all the earth, bringing your truth, your justice, and your peace to all the world. Lord, we are so slow to understand what your Word and your presence as one born to us of the woman Mary and of our Father God in the power of the Spirit means for our own bodies and communities, let alone the whole world. Intercede for us and pray with us that your Father and our Father's kingdom will come on earth as it is in heaven, in us, today. Amen."

THE THIRD GLORIOUS MYSTERY:

Pentecost—the Father Sends the Spirit upon the Church

SCRIPTURE

All of these the eleven apostles together gave themselves to constant prayer. With them were some women and also Mary, the mother of Jesus, and his brothers. (Acts 1:14)

Then the day of Pentecost came, they were all together in one place. And suddenly out of the sky came a sound like a strong rushing wind and it filled the whole house where they were sitting. There appeared tongues as if of fire which parted and came to rest upon each one of them. All were filled with the Holy Spirit and began to speak other languages, as the Spirit enabled them to speak. (Acts 2:1–4)

Or,

As for the eleven disciples, they went to

Galilee, to the mountain where Jesus had told them to go. When they saw Jesus, they bowed before him, although some doubted.

Then Jesus approached them and said, "I have been given all authority in heaven and on earth. Go, therefore, and make disciples from all nations. Baptize them in the Name of the Father and of the Son and of the Holy Spirit, and teach them to fulfill all that I have commanded you. I am with you always until the end of the world. (Matthew 27:16–20)

> *Christ was himself but one and lived and died*
> *   but once;*
> *but the Holy Ghost makes of every Christian*
> *   another Christ,*
> *an After Christ, lives a million lives in every age.*
>
> —GERARD MANLEY HOPKINS

There are so many names and images for this gift of God, the Holy Spirit, the third person of the Trinity. The word *person,* from the Latin, means "per"—through— and *sonare,* "to sound," so person means "to sound through." This image of God is how we hear, through whom we know and understand, and with whom we live the Word and the will of the Father God, in the person of Jesus incarnate and risen. The Spirit speaks, sings, whispers, enlightens, frees, instills courage, gives meaning, opens our ears and eyes, penetrates, transforms, and empowers us as once this same Spirit did the person of Jesus. The Spirit speaks now in us, in believers, and in the Church—and for those who have the ears to hear, in everything. The voice of the Spirit sounds a clarion call in refugees, the homeless, the victims of violence and war, the children and the old; in the weather patterns that change because of human beings' choices; in the events of history; in politics, economics, other religions, cultures; and in prophets.

The person of the Spirit is described in terms of the senses of human beings—hearing, speaking, smelling, tasting, touching—and in the images that accompany these experiences: voice, sound, silence, word, music, odor, scent, sweetness, sharpness, caress, warmth, light, fire, wind, air, breath. With this outpouring of the Spirit as gift to us, the Spirit now seeks to work in us as the Spirit compelled Jesus in power. In the most powerful resurrection account, we see, hear, and feel the breath and spirit of Jesus upon the community: "Again Jesus said to them: 'Peace be with you. As the Father has sent me, so I send you.' After saying this he breathed on them and said to them, 'Receive the Holy Spirit, for those whose sins you forgive, they are forgiven; for those whose sins you retain, they are retained.' " (John 20:21–23)

With this "first gift given to those who believe" (third Eucharist prayer) the power to forgive sin and the power to hold bound those who do evil is shared with the followers of Jesus and the Church. Earlier, at the Last Supper, Jesus told his friends that his presence would remain with them in the gift of the Spirit of Truth, as Paraclete (as one who stands by your side), as an advocate (as in a court of law), as comforter and protector (we will not be left bereft as orphans). Jesus describes the Spirit as witness to all that he is, says, and does and we are to be imitators and witnesses in that same Spirit. (John 15:26) This Spirit "whom the Father will send in my name will teach you all things and remind you of all that I have told you. Peace be with you: I give you my peace. Not as the world gives peace do I give it to you. Do not be troubled; do not be afraid." (John 14:22–27)

This Spirit is a new presence of Jesus with us. In the early Church, this Spirit was sometimes described as the shadow of Jesus bent over his disciples, as constant companion and guest within as well as a presence without.

With this gift, the Spirit speaks in those who believe in Jesus. The Spirit speaks to Philip (Acts 8:29); to Peter (Acts 10:19 and 11:12); to the community gathered in prayer as they deliberate what actions to take in the Church (Acts 13:2); and through others to Paul in Caesarea (Acts 21:11); and on numerous other occasions. Not surprisingly, one of the strongest characteristics of the Spirit when it comes and settles upon the gathered community is the gift of languages so that others can understand the Scriptures, in their own language: "All were filled with the Holy Spirit and began to speak other languages, as the Spirit enabled them to speak. Staying in Jerusalem were religious Jews from every nation under heaven. When they heard this sound, a crowd gathered, all excited because each heard them speaking in his own language." (Acts 2:4–6)

The Spirit is about communication, dialogue, understanding, communion, diversity, and unity and is given to believers to draw together all peoples and nations under heaven. In the last lines of the Gospel of Matthew, this is absolutely clear, and it is issued as a command as Jesus shares the power that has been given to him by the Father, through the Spirit. As the Spirit is given to speak the truth, to forgive sin, and to hold the world bound and accountable for sin, evil, and injustice, so the Spirit is given to "make disciples, to baptize and to teach all that Jesus taught to those who come after him." With the gift of the Spirit, all believers and the Church become missionary and respectful of all nations, cultures, languages, genders, and expressions of being human and being holy.

Church begins with preaching, and modeling belief into practice within the community, and then extends out in liturgy, compassion for the poor, the call to conversion, and incorporation into the community of believers. But this work of the Church must happen side by side with the transformation of society and nations. The Spirit does not just suggest or ask; the Spirit demands, compels, and drives those who have known its touch out into the world to confront evil and to bring the kingdom of God to bear upon every reality in the world. This gift of the Spirit is for making Christians, healing and strengthening the Church, and for sourcing the power that will make the new creation visible for all peoples to see and experience. The Spirit is our source of unity, integrity, communion, hope, freedom, courage, enlightenment, compassion, and justice.

The vitality and imagination of the inner life of the Church is intimately bound up with its work on behalf of the poor, for justice, and for prophetically speaking the truth to the nations of the world. The night before he was murdered, Martin Luther King, Jr. spoke to his people, rallying them to stand firm in their belief and commitment to nonviolent transformation. In the book *A Testament of Hope,* he spoke of the fire hoses that had been turned on those gathered to speak the truth in Birmingham; "There was a certain kind of fire that no water could put out . . . We had known water. If we were Baptists or some other denomination, we had been immersed. If we were Methodists, and some others, we had been sprinkled, but we knew water." And as we have known water, we have known fire too!

John Paul II in his encyclical letter *Redemptoris Mission 2* has written, "Faith is strengthened when it is given to others." Our faith is called to be universal, seeded in every language and culture, nation, and people so that the richness and diversity of God can be seen, honored, and known ever more fully. Jesus' own words demand that believers be present in every situation, especially those of injustice, lack, and violence so that the Word of truth and hope might be offered and given as gift to all. That gift of the Spirit is both abiding and prophetic, enduring with faith, grace, and the radical demand for conversion and accompaniment by the poor and those who seek God's kingdom of justice and peace. We are commanded to go out, make disciples, baptize, and teach the Good News, but at the same time to see the presence of the Spirit of God there ahead of us. Bishop Kenneth Cragg wrote to his church: "Our first task in approaching another people, another culture, another religion, is to take off our shoes for the place we are approaching is holy. Else we may find ourselves treading on people's dreams. More seriously still, we may forget that God was there before our arrival." ("What Makes a Missionary?" Alice Keenleyside, MHM, *Priests and People*, October 1996, p. 372)

All this work of the Spirit is about completing what God has begun in Jesus. Now we are called upon to work together, as we are sent out into the world, to continue what has been begun and to let the Spirit work in us for the healing of all nations and the uncovering and extending of the kingdom that arrived in the person and presence of Jesus among us. Yet this working of the Spirit is always in the present, demanding that we witness to God's work in the world now, here, in our place. With the gift of the Spirit we are reminded that with our God there are no boundaries, no borders, no nations, no kingdom but that of God's forgiving mercy, and peace born of justice that is not like any version of the world's peace. There are endless gifts and works of the Spirit and a multitude of ways to express this Spirit of Jesus present with us still, and always. A mystic of the late Middle Ages, Hildegard of Bingen, writes, "The Holy Spirit is the life that gives life, moving all things. It is the root in every creature and purifys all things, wiping away our sins, anointing wounds. It is radiant life, worthy of practice, awakening and enlivening all things."

And there are ancient liturgical ways to know the Spirit. These lines are selected from the sequence "Veni, Sancte Spiritus," sung on the feast of Pentecost.

> *Come, Holy Spirit, come! And from your celestial home*
> *Shed a ray of light divine!*
> *Come, Father of the poor!*
> *Come, source of all our store!*
> *You, of comforters the best; you, the soul's most welcome guest;*
> *Sweet refreshment here below, in our labor, rest most sweet;*
> *Grateful coolness in the heat; solace in the midst of woe.*
> *Where you are not; we have naught,*
> *Nothing good in deed or thought; nothing free from taint of ill.*
> *Heal our wounds, our strength renew;*
> *On our dryness pour your dew;*
> *Bend the stubborn heart and will; melt the frozen, warm the chill.*
> *Guide the steps that go astray.*
> *On the faithful who adore and confess you, evermore*
> *In your sevenfold gift descend;*
> *Give them your salvation, Lord;*
> *Give them joys that never end. Amen. Alleluia.*

It is important to remember that the Spirit is first of all given to the community, when believers gather together and pray together. In Matthew's account the women witness to the men and then all the disciples gather on the mountaintop; some believe and others doubt. In the Gospel of John, Jesus comes to the upper room and breaks in on a threatened and fearful group of disheartened followers with the command and blessing of peace that they are to bring into the world with courage and joy. And Luke, in both Acts and his gospel, draws together at the beginning and the end of the text those who are witness to what Jesus has said and done. He names specifically all the disciples, minus Judas, and then mentions those who have been with Jesus since the beginning of his ministry: "with them were some women and also Mary, the mother of Jesus, and his brothers." (Acts 1:13–14) Some of these women are named earlier—Mary of Magdala, Joanna, Susanna, and others (Luke 8:1–3)—and in the account of the crucifixion and resurrection another is added: Mary, the mother of James. Luke begins with Mary, as the first to hear the Word of God spoken in flesh. She is present with the rest of the community that will be the Church when the Spirit comes upon all who believe in Jesus. The Spirit makes these believers the Church, a community where gender, blood relations, social status, age, race, geography, nation, and marriage are not foundational. What is essential is hearing, believing, and putting the Word into practice by becoming a disciple, picking up your cross, and following in the mission of Jesus. Everyone who believes is seized by the Spirit! It is a universal gift given by the generosity of God and can come suddenly like a furious spring rain or continuously in a slow, soft rain that soaks just as thoroughly anyone caught in its falling. Everyone born of this water and Spirit are initiated into a lifelong process of conversion, transformation, mission, and holiness that is dynamic, demanding, freeing, and expressive.

With the mention of Mary, the mother of Jesus, among those who received the Spirit, we see where Mary belongs: among us, as one of us. The portrait of Mary that is found in both the beginning and end of Luke seeks to reveal something of import in God that is essential to the revelation of who our God is and how we are all loved. Marie-Louise Gubler writes in *Theology Today,*

> For Luke, Mary cannot be separated from those women and men who placed their hope in Jesus and whose journey ended in the darkness of Good Friday but led to the astonishing turn after Easter and Pentecost. For Luke, the favored one of the beginning (Luke 1:28) cannot be separated from the favored criminal of Jesus' last minutes ("Today you will be with me in paradise" [Luke 23:42]). Mary's song proclaims that the grace of the first and the last hour are equal expressions of God's mercy. ("Luke's Portrait of Mary," TD 36,1 [Spring 1989], pp. 19–24)

This is the mother of Jesus' place in the church, in history and in the world—with all the other believers and followers of the Word made flesh who dwells among us still. John Paul II writes of this mystery of Pentecost in his reflections in "On the Most Holy Rosary":

The contemplation of this scene, like that of the other glorious mysteries, ought to lead the faithful to an ever greater appreciation of their new life in Christ, lived in the heart of the Church, a life of which the scene of Pentecost itself is the great "icon." The glorious mysteries thus lead the faithful to greater hope for the eschatological goal toward which they journey as members of the pilgrim people of God in history. This can only impel them to bear courageous witness to that "good news" which gives meaning to their entire existence. (RVM, #23)

Pentecost bestows upon us the glory of God, the Spirit of God, the power and mission of God, and we are commanded to bring the Word of God in our words and our flesh out into the whole world, making disciples of the Word, in the image of the Trinity, and instructing new Christians to be the light and truth of Jesus, the beloved of God, in their baptismal faith and lives so that all the earth sees the wonder of our God.

Let us pray. "Father, you sent the Holy Spirit upon those marked out to be your children and you stir into flame the fire of faith and truth that was seeded in us by our baptism and confirmation. You make our hearts burn with fresh insight and understanding every time we gather and listen to your Scriptures and gather around your Word made flesh in our midst in the Eucharist. You graciously remember us in your mercy by always forgiving us. And you breathe passion and grace into our weary hearts, encouraging us to forget ourselves in the service of others and the preaching of your Word to others. And in all times and places you desire to make us one in you, who are Father, Son, and Spirit. Come! Come! Always come! and touch our hearts of flesh with your presence, your Word, your breath and life so our presence may be your presence in the world. Amen."

THE FOURTH AND FIFTH GLORIOUS MYSTERIES:

In recent traditions, the fourth and fifth glorious mysteries of the Rosary are entitled the Assumption of Mary, and the Crowning of Mary as Queen of the Angels and Saints. In John Paul II's recent Apostolic Letter, "On the Most Holy Rosary," he speaks generally of Mary's joy and the intense experience of the Risen Lord she must have known in her life, sharing in that same glory, knowing the privilege and the destiny reserved for all the just at the resurrection of the dead. And she is seen as "the anticipation and the supreme realization of the eschatological state of the Church." However, at the end of the description of the glorious mysteries, he writes:

The cycles of meditation proposed by the Holy Rosary are by no means exhaustive, but they do bring to mind what is essential, and they awaken in the soul a thirst for a knowledge of Christ continually nourished by the pure source of the Gospel. Every individual event in the life of Christ, as narrated by the evangelists, is resplendent with the Mystery that surpasses all understanding (cf. Ephesians 3:19): the Mystery of the Word made flesh, in whom "all the fullness of God dwells bodily" (Colossians 2:9). . . . The Letter to the Ephesians makes this heartfelt prayer for all the baptized: "May Christ dwell in your hearts through faith, so that you, being rooted and grounded in love, may have power . . . to know the love of Christ which surpasses knowledge, that you may be filled with all the fullness of God" (3:17–19).

In light of this statement and in accord with the emphasis that the mysteries are about the person of Jesus and the Word of God in the Scriptures, two other glorious mysteries will be included here that continue the revelation about the heart of our faith. We will look at the belief of the Coming of Christ in Glory as the Son of Man and the ultimate mystery of the Trinity as more indicative of the belief of the Church. A short reflection on the teachings about Mary in the larger context of faith will be presented, followed by the deeper reflection and emphasis on the continuing revelation of Jesus Christ, the Son of Man, and the Trinity.

THE ASSUMPTION OF MARY

SCRIPTURE

Then his mother and his relatives came to him, but they could not get to him because of the crowd. Someone told him, "Your mother and your brothers are standing outside and wish to meet you." Then Jesus answered, "My mother and my brothers are those who hear the word of God and do it." (Luke 8:19–21)

Or,

Then his mother and his brothers came. As they stood outside, they sent someone to call him. The crowd sitting around Jesus told him, "Your mother and brothers are outside asking for you." He replied, "Who are my mother and my brothers?" And looking around at those who sat there he said, "Here are my mother and my brothers. Whoever does the will of God is brother and sister and mother to me." (Mark 3:31–35)

> *"Rejoice, Mother of Light: Jesus, the sun of justice, overcoming the darkness of the tomb, sheds his radiance over the whole world, Alleluia."*

—FROM *COMMUNION ANTIPHON FOR THE MASS, MARY AND THE RESURRECTION OF THE LORD* (A SPECIAL COLLECTION OF MASSES, 1986)

In the gospel traditions of Mark, Matthew, and Luke, the only times that the mother of Jesus is mentioned in the heart of these texts are in these statements and again, indirectly, in Luke, when a woman in a crowd cries out in praise, "Blessed is the womb that bore you." (Luke 11:27–28) But even then Jesus will not allow that statement to stand as spoken. He replies in contradiction and concordance: "Blessed rather are those who hear the word of God and keep it." Mary is included in that group that hears and obeys the word of God. She belongs to those who are intimate and close with him, in his new family that is based, not on blood ties, biology, or race and nation, but on obedience, belief, and a share in his sufferings, and so in his glory.

In Acts, the description of the community is more extended than the actual experience of the coming of the Spirit upon them. The three groups are named: the men disciples by name, minus Judas, who betrayed Jesus, and Matthias, who will be chosen by lot; together with the women and Mary, the mother of Jesus; and his brothers. His blood family is mentioned last. The more essential mark of the community is that "All these with one accord devoted themselves to prayer." This is the criteria for the reception of the Spirit, the sharing in the resurrection and glory of Jesus and the intimacy with God, which must be shared with others.

In his Apostolic Letter, John Paul writes about a "secret" that is in service to the ideal of all those who are baptized into Christ. He calls it "Mary's way," describing it in these words.

> It is the way of the example of the Virgin of Nazareth, a woman of faith, of silence, of attentive listening. It is also the way of a Marian devotion inspired by knowledge of the inseparable bond between Christ and his Blessed Mother; the mysteries of Christ are also in some sense the mysteries of his Mother, even when they do not involve her directly, for she lives from him and through him. By making our own the words of the Angel Gabriel and Saint Elizabeth contained in the Hail Mary, we find ourselves constantly drawn to seek out afresh in Mary, in her arms and in her heart, the "blessed fruit of her womb." (cf. Luke 1:42)

This is a good description of Mary: a woman of faith, of silence, and of attentive listening. And it is about devotion that must be seen to honor and respect the Scriptures, the Word of God as primary. More than the words of the Hail Mary, the Word of the Scriptures reveals the mystery of Christ. The inseparable bond between Christ and his mother is, in the words of Jesus himself, to be seen in the context of the inseparable bond among Christ and his true mothers, sisters, and brothers, his family of disciples born in Word, water, blood, and Spirit. This is his Church, the bond of Spirit between Christ and all those who believe in his words and seek to put them into practice—all of us marvelously given intimacy with our God in Jesus that is stronger, deeper, and truer by far than the intimacy between mother and child.

Bishop Kallistos of Diokleia, an Orthodox bishop, wrote in *The Tablet* (January 17, 1998), "The mystery of [Christ's] Mother forms part of the Church's inner, secret tradition, that is revealed only through prayer and doxology to those inside the Church." This may be true, but intimacy and holiness in this family is not based on domestic or familial qualities as found in families in Western cultures. Whatever the Church says of Mary, it says of every believer, every Christian, and every disciple described by Jesus as "his mother, sister and brother." This is not just our hope, but it is our baptized reality, our calling as disciples, and our promise. We will all know communion with God, joy in God's presence, because we have believed the Word that was spoken to us; because we brought forth that Word into our lives and world; because we have stood faithfully at the foot of the cross; and because we obey Christ's mandate to go into the world with the Good News of forgiveness and mercy, bringing the truth and the peace of God to those who are most in need of this compassionate new family.

Let us pray. "Jesus, you invite us into your new family and call us mother, sister, and brother, giving us your first gift of the Spirit so that we can, together with you, call God our Father. Your mother stands with us in the love and intimacy of being disciple, witness, and friend, obedient to your Word. May we honor you, O God, first and foremost with all our hearts, and souls, and minds, and resources and so honor your mother by being your beloved children along with Jesus your son. We ask this in your own Spirit every moment of our lives until we know you in your glory forever. Amen."

THE CORONATION OF MARY: QUEEN OF THE ANGELS AND SAINTS

SCRIPTURE

Well now, if you obey in truth the voice of Yahweh, your God, practicing and observing all the commandments which I give to you today, Yahweh, your God, shall raise you high above all the nations of the earth. Then all these blessings shall reach you and come upon you for having obeyed the voice of Yahweh, your God.

Blessed shall you be in the city and in the field. Blessed shall be the fruit of your body and the fruit of your land, the young of your asses, the offspring of your cattle and sheep. Blessed shall be your basket and your bowl of dough. Blessed shall you be when you begin and when you finish.

. . . Yahweh will make you a holy people, as he has sworn, if you keep his commands and follow in his ways. Then all the nations of the earth

shall see that you are under the protection of
Yahweh and they will respect you. Yahweh shall
fill you with all kinds of good things, increasing
the fruit of your womb, the fruit of your livestock
and the fruit of your land which Yahweh promised on oath to your fathers that he would give
you. (Deuteronomy 28:1–6, 9–11)

Or,

My daughter, may the Most High God bless
you more than all the women on earth. And
blessed be the Lord God, the Creator of heaven
and earth, who has led you to behead the leader
of our enemies.

Never will people forget the confidence you
have shown; they will always remember the power
of God. May God ensure your everlasting glory,
and may he reward and bless you for you have
risked your life when your race was humiliated.
You chose instead to do the best before God in
order to prevent our downfall. And all the people said: "Amen! Amen!" (Judith 13:18–20)

Or,

Mary then set out for a town in the hills of
Judah. She entered the house of Zechariah and
greeted Elizabeth. When Elizabeth heard Mary's
greeting the baby leapt in her womb. Elizabeth
was filled with the Holy Spirit, and giving a loud
cry, said, "You are most blessed among women
and blessed is the fruit of your womb! How is it
that the mother of my Lord comes to me? The
moment your greeting sounded in my ears, the

baby within me leapt for joy. Blessed are you who believed that the Lord's word would come true." (Luke 1:39–45)

O Mary, chariot of fire, you bore the fire hidden and veiled under the ashes of your humanness.

—CATHERINE OF SIENA

Especially during the Middle Ages, devotion to Mary as a queen developed, modeled on that toward actual queens of Western Christendom and before then, the empresses of the East. In the seventeenth century, a special rite was designed for the coronation of religious images of Jesus, Mary, and the saints, and in 1981 new rites were devised. But there is nothing in the Scriptures that images the mother of Jesus as a queen, either on earth or in heaven. In fact, they reveal a woman who would fall into an utterly opposite category. She was poor, from a town far in the north, away from Jerusalem. She lived in occupied territory and under foreign domination her whole life, as a refugee, illegal alien, displaced person. She was a widow for a good portion of her life, and watched her son tortured and executed by the dominant empire that ruled her world. She was ordinary in every sense, yet she belonged to a faithful remnant of Israel that longed for the coming of the one who would set Israel free and turn the hearts of the people back to their God.

She is seen in Luke's gospel in the tradition of valiant women who served their people and their God, rising to respond to their need. Elizabeth's greeting and Mary's response in the opening words of the Magnificat follow these stories and ways of praising people and God very closely. The song that Mary sings in response to Elizabeth's prophetic cry of recognition, first of the child she bears who is the Lord and then of the fact that she believes and is obedient to the Word of God, is also formed in the prophetic tradition. It is a song of revolution, or of revolutions: of one's own pride and sin; of social, political, and economic upheaval. This song is an announcement, a prelude of the gospel's reversal of all values and overturning of structures, the raising up of the poor and the faithful as a blessing of the mercy God has shown to his people since Abraham's first covenant. Mary is seized by the Spirit and sings her song of the glories that God will mysteriously bring to pass in the world in the person of Jesus, her child, but a child that is born of God and so belongs to all the people and eventually will be seen to belong to all nations, not just the Jewish people.

Everything in the Gospels is about human life, day-to-day events and experiences, from the most difficult and trying—being without children, living as slaves in one's own country—to moments of surprise in washing feet, banquet feasts, lepers, illness, hunger, and hospitality. It is life on earth and the Gospels proclaim that God is here on earth and we find God in one another, in flesh and blood and, strangely, in the poor, in suffering, and in all those places it is hard to see God's presence among us: in the grave, torture, even the "groaning of the earth itself" (Romans 8). God is here, down-to-earth, touched here, worshiped here, and obeyed here first. You don't have to look in the heavens anymore. God now speaks to us, as once he did with Moses, Elijah, and others. At the end of the Luke's gospel the angels even question the men of Galilee: "Why do you stand looking up to heaven?" (Acts 1:10)

In Luke, Mary's faith, like ours, begins with a decision and will entail a lifetime process of continual choices for conversion, change, understanding, and growth before it develops into an Easter faith, just as it was with other disciples. Her greatness and her holiness, like our own, lie not in motherhood or fatherhood but in faith, in obedience, and in endurance until our deaths, no matter what we are called to face and experience.

It is the letters of Timothy, of James and John in Revelation, where the image of the crown is found, not in the Gospels. And all of the references are bound to the demand for faithfulness, of enduring suffering, persecution, and even martyrdom for our belief in Jesus and the practice of that belief publicly. In the second letter to Timothy, Paul writes of saying good-bye to his friend and disciple as he faces his "time of sacrifice." It is fraught with sadness and bittersweet joy: "I have fought the good fight, I have finished the race, I have kept the faith. Now there is laid up for me the crown of righteousness with which the Lord, the just judge, will reward me on that day; and not only me, but all those who have longed for his glorious coming." (2 Timothy 4:7–8)

James writes to his community in the same vein: "Happy are those who patiently endure trials, because afterwards they will receive the crown of life which the Lord promised to those who love him." (James 1:12) This is the beatitude of James for his church, much as Elizabeth blessed Mary and all those who believe in the Word of God and obey. The allusions to crowns are all found in these exhortations to those who are left behind as others face departures or death. Peter writes to his church, describing himself as an elder, a witness to the sufferings of Jesus, and someone who has tried to be a good shepherd. He exhorts those in authority to guard their people with a generous heart and not lord it over them. Instead they are to be an example. "Then, when the Good Shepherd appears, you will be given a crown of unfading glory." (1 Peter 5:4)

Last, in the book of Revelation, it is the angel that speaks to John so that he might give hope and courage to so many who are being persecuted, tortured, and martyred for their faith. The angel speaks: "Remain faithful even to death and I will give you the crown of life." (Revelation 2:10) This is the crown that will be given to all who are faithful, not any worldly crown found in the places of power on earth.

In the ritual of crowning a statue or image of Mary, this is the prayer that is suggested.

Mary, Virgin for ever.
Most worthy Queen of the world,
pray for our peace and salvation,
for you are the Mother of Christ,
the Lord and Savior of all.

If Mary is a queen, perhaps it would be better if she was seen to walk the earth, among the poor, with those who struggle daily for survival, and with the prophets who seek justice and peace for all upon whom God's favor rests, as she did when she lived on earth. The image of Our Lady of Guadalupe, an indigenous woman of a race enslaved by militant believers, with her bare feet planted firmly on the earth, calling for reconciliation, justice, and compassion for the victims of violence, is the only woman of courage and prophecy that our earth needs today. Our God is here, on earth, until he comes again in glory as the Son of Man, the Just Judge of the nations.

Let us pray. "Father, your son Jesus, the Crucified One told us that we would have to bear our share of the burden of the gospel, and perhaps stand up for what we believe, witnessing to your truth. To witness is to be a martyr, our last statement of belief, laying down our lives to proclaim the truth. The crowns of courage and endurance, of grace and obedience, of resistance to evil without harming anyone, and of peace and reconciliation, of compassion and mercy, are the gifts of a life handed over to your kingdom that you brought to earth in Jesus, Son of God, and son of Mary. May we be your peacemakers who build your kingdom on earth so clearly that all know we are citizens of your universal kingdom of the poor, of justice and of mercy. May we seek to gift one another with your glory here on earth in the works of compassion and forgiveness until you come in glory to crown all our efforts with your blessing. Father, we ask this grace, all of us who are, with Mary, your beloved children, born of your Spirit and your Word made flesh. Amen."

 ## THE FOURTH GLORIOUS MYSTERY:

The Coming of the Son of Man in Glory to Judge the Nations with Justice

SCRIPTURES

When Jesus saw Nathanael coming, he said of him, "Here comes an Israelite, a true one; there is nothing false in him." Nathanael asked him, "How do you know me?" And Jesus said to him, "Before Philip called you, you were under the fig tree and I saw you."

Nathanael answered, "Master, you are the Son of God! You are the King of Israel!" But Jesus replied, "You believe because I said: I saw you under the fig tree. But you will see greater things than that. Truly, I say to you, you will see the heavens opened and the angels of God as-

cending and descending upon the Son of Man."
(John 1:47–51)

Or,

Jesus began to teach them that the Son of
Man had to suffer many things and be rejected by
the elders, the chief priests and the teachers of
the Law. He would be killed and after three days
rise again. Jesus said all these things quite openly,
so that Peter took him aside and began to protest
strongly. But Jesus turning around, and looking
at his disciples, rebuked Peter, saying, "Get behind me, Satan! You are thinking, not as God
does, but as people do." (Mark 8:31–33 and cf.
Mark 9:30–32)

Or,

On hearing this, the other ten were angry
with James and John; Jesus then called them to
him and said, "As you know, the so-called rulers
of the nations act as tyrants and their great ones
oppress them. But it shall not be so among you;
whoever would be great among you must be your
servant, and whoever would be first among you
shall make himself the slave of all. Think of the
Son of Man who has not come to be served but to
serve and to give his life to redeem many. (Mark
10:41–45)

> *Each mortal thing does one thing and the same:*
> *Deals out that being indoors each one dwells;*
> *Selves—goes itself; myself it speaks and spells,*
> *Crying What I do is me: for that I came.*

I say more: the just man justices;
Keeps grace: that keeps all his goings graces;
Acts in God's eye what in God's eye he is—
Christ—for Christ plays in ten thousand places,
Lovely in limbs, and lovely in eyes not his
To the Father through the features of men's faces.

GERARD MANLEY HOPKINS,
"THE SOLDIER," *THE WORKS*
OF GERARD MANLEY HOPKINS
(WORDSWORTH EDITIONS, 1994)

This title, the Son of Man, is the phrase that Jesus uses to describe himself in all the Gospels, most especially in Mark, Matthew, and Luke. This is Jesus' own vision of who he is and what he has been sent into the world to do, in obedience to his Father. It is an image that many are not familiar with though it is found so often in the holy texts. The image is found in the book of Daniel. Daniel is given a series of visions that are frightening and terrifying. They detail the destruction of Jerusalem, the Temple, and the people's dreams as they are driven into exile and slavery to Babylon. They are visions of judgment and the consequences of the people's arrogance, their defiance of the prophets' call to repentance, and their disobedience to the covenant. This is one of the first visions of Daniel.

I looked and saw the following:
Some thrones were set in place and One of Great Age took his seat. His robe was white as

snow, his hair white as washed wool. His throne was flames of fire with wheels of blazing fire. A river of fire sprang forth and flowed before him. Thousands upon thousands served him and a countless multitude stood before him. Those in the tribunal took their seats and opened the book.

. . . I continued watching the nocturnal vision:

One like a son of man came on the clouds of heaven. He faced the One of Great Age and was brought into his presence.

Dominion, honor and kingship were given him, and all the peoples and nations of every language served him. His dominion is eternal and shall never pass away; his kingdom will never be destroyed. (Daniel 7:1–10, 13–14)

This vision of "one like a Son of man" comes in the midst of visions of four beasts that devour and destroy the world and its peoples, dominating the earth with evil. The fourth beast with a great horn was waging war against "the holy ones and subduing them until the One of Great Age came to do justice for the holy ones of the Most High, and the time came for the holy ones to take possession of the kingdom." (Daniel 7:21) When Daniel asks for an explanation of what is happening he is told that there will be suffering, persecution, and terrible death, but the day will come when justice will be done and that God's dominion will rule the earth. He is told that one day, "The kingship, dominion and leadership of all the kingdoms of the world shall be given to the holy ones of God Most High; his kingdom will be without end. All kingdoms will serve him and be subject to him." (Daniel 7:26–27)

This vision comes again and causes Daniel great anguish because of the things of the earth: wars, pestilence, drought, greed, arrogance, lies, disdain for the covenant and the poor, injustice, and violence. But just when it seems darkest, Daniel is given another sight that rouses his heart and lifts his soul: "Then all those whose names are written in the Book will be saved. Many of those who sleep in the Region of the Dust will awake, some to everlasting life but others to eternal horror and shame. Those who acquired knowledge will shine like the brilliance of the firmament; those who taught people to be just will shine like the stars for all eternity." (Daniel 12:1b–3)

"One like a son of man" is a liberator from anguish, suffering, injustice, persecution, and despair while being also the one who judges all nations justly. The One of Great Age is a way of referring to God, and the other figure is a human being. Jesus, when questioned by the high priest at his interrogation before being handed over to Pilate, answers who he is with these words: So the High Priest said to him, "In the name of the living God, I command you to tell us: Are you the Messiah, the Son of God?" Jesus answered, "It is just as you say. I tell you more: from now on, you will see the Son of Man seated at the right hand of the Most Powerful God and coming on the clouds of heaven." (Matthew 26:63–64)

Jesus answers the high priest by saying, "It is you who use those words, not me." Jesus refuses to accept the terms "Messiah" and "Son of God" because that was the usual way the Jews signified the kings and saviors of Israel in the past. He is Savior, but not in the ways of kingdoms of this earth. This is what Jesus is trying to tell his disciples in Mark (and Matthew and Luke as well). He tries again and again to get them, and us, to understand that he will overcome the world by suffering and death. Three times in as many chapters he tells them that he will be rejected, handed over to be tortured, crucified, and on the third day, rise. They do not want to hear it. Peter, as spokesman, not only resists but tries to rebuke Jesus. And it is Jesus who turns on all of them, calling them Satan because they are thinking in terms of the kingdoms of this world and not as God thinks and acts. The word *Satan* literally means "the Hinderer." A point is reached where even Jesus' own disciples become what seeks to hinder him from going to Jerusalem, speaking the truth of the gospel, and laying down his life in forgiveness, courage, and love.

Jesus speaks of his suffering, and that is what registers with the disciples. But he also speaks of rising, of glory that God will confer on him because of his faithfulness. This phrase "and on the third day" was traditionally used as a formula that indicates a time of terrible suffering, but after that would come salvation from God. Jesus does tell them he is going to die—terribly, at the hands of Imperial Rome—but he also tells them of his trust in God no matter what happens to him. Jesus faces what awaits him in Jerusalem, the fate of all the prophets, but he faces it with hope in God who will be with him to save him in mercy. The gospel is clear that following Jesus can be very dangerous and it will be tempting to deny Jesus—as all the disciples do at Jesus' arrest. Jesus tells us that if we are not to be caught denying him, we must begin the discipline of denying ourselves so that we will faithfully follow him to the cross and to resurrection. Jesus himself is bearing witness to life, death, and resurrection.

The disciples catch bits and pieces of what Jesus is saying and they want the glory but not the path that leads to it through suffering because of being associated with Jesus. And so James and John separate themselves from the band of disciples and attempt to procure, through the intercession of their mother, what they perceive to be the best positions in Jesus' coming kingdom. When the others find out, they are enraged. Dissension and self-interest begin to divide them. Again, Jesus tries to teach all who would claim to be his own that his ways are not like those of the world. His power and his authority are expressed in service, in surrender and obedience and lowliness, in meekness (the word means nonviolence), humility, and literally giving oneself as a ransom for many.

Jesus is as blunt as he can be with them. If you want to rise in his company, then you must bend low, serve others, and obey God's will for justice for the poor, for peace and reconciliation and freedom among those who need it the most. And this can bring with it suffering and death, as it will for Jesus. The two seats of honor and distinction that they coveted are not his to give. Those seats will go to the two thieves who are crucified with him. One will know the kingdom of God the day he perishes; the other decides against Jesus and curses him along with those on the ground watching Jesus die.

This is the Son of Man. He is the Crucified One, resisted and betrayed even by his own friends and followers. This is, in the words of John the Baptist, the Lamb of God, reminiscent of the blood of the lamb smeared on the doorposts of the Israelites as they waited through the long night of the first Passover for the angel of death. They were saved by the blood of the lamb. This too is the Lamb of the Book of Revelation, the only one worthy to break open the seals of the scroll and read out the names of those who are saved. (Revelation 5:9–10) This is the prophet-preacher Jesus, who broke all the laws, touching lepers, the unclean, the sick, sinners, and those who were pushed to the margins of society by those who made and kept the rules. This is Jesus, the truth of the mercy and compassion of God, who will come to judge the nations with justice, when the time is fulfilled and he returns in glory. He is a human being that has known terrible injustice inflicted on his body, but that is what gives him the power to judge all nations justly.

This is the Jesus of the famous story in Matthew 25, separating out the sheep and the goats using the criteria of how we have treated the "least of our brothers and sisters"—because in effect, that is how we have treated our God made flesh among us. The Last Judgment story sets up the work of the Son of Man when he comes in glory with startling simplicity, demanding integrity and justice be done in the presence of all the nations: "When the Son of Man comes in his glory with all his angels, he will sit on the throne of his Glory. All the nations will be brought before him, and as a shepherd separates the sheep from the goats, so will he do with them, placing the sheep on his right and the goats on his left." (Matthew 25:31–33)

Those who know the Son of Man in the person of those who are hungry, thirsty, a stranger in need of shelter and clothing, the sick and imprisoned, and treat them with justice and human kindness will be called "the blessed of my Father" and welcomed into the kingdom of God. And those that refuse their fellow human beings, those in most dire need of the basic necessities of human existence—food, shelter, clothing, medical care, dignity, another chance at freedom and life—will be named as those so insensitive to others' needs, so selfish and unjust, that they will be herded off from the presence of God. Jesus is teaching that our human deeds, our choices in regard to other human beings, reveal our own humanity, our belief in God, our worship, and our salvation. We have only two choices in the world: to look with love or to look with disdain upon others, especially the poor and those in need and our enemies. Those who choose to be inhuman on earth are judged by the Son of Man, the

most fully human being, the beloved child of God, Jesus.
And those who choose to live as human beings, careful of
others and so obedient to God's will that all know ever
more abundant life, will be blessed with the presence of
God. Being human, being just, being compassionate,
being of service to others, giving what others' need and
treating then with dignity, saves us forever. When Jesus
tells this parable, he is ready to turn and go into
Jerusalem. The gospel continues: "When Jesus had finished all he wanted to say, he told his disciples, 'You know
that in two days' time it will be the Passover and the Son
of Man will be handed over to be crucified.' " (Matthew
26:1–2)

The work of Jesus on earth is finished and he turns
toward his crucifixion and death, trusting in his Father to
save him. And when the Father raises him from the dead
he will pass on this work and his power to those who follow him. We are to bring God's kingdom of justice for the
poor and to treat all with dignity, even our enemies, as
though they were the body of Christ, and we are to put
into practice forgiveness and the command to "love one
another as I have loved you" toward all human beings.
This is our life, and everlasting life depends on it.

This is how Jesus sees himself and how the gospel
presents him. One day Jesus, the Son of Man, the
Crucified and Risen One, will come again to judge all the
nations and peoples with justice. He will come in God's
glory to do justice for all the earth and to make known the
hearts of all peoples and nations. We will know and be

seen for what we are: either the friends of God who touched all human beings with the compassion we have known in Jesus, or we will condemn ourselves to isolation from God by our refusal to teach other human beings the goodness that our God has shown to us. We will all stand in the presence of God, in the presence of the Holy One of God, the Son of Man, and be known, be seen for what we have always been, and all the children of the earth will know where we have stood and to whom we have bowed down. We will choose every day of our lives either to bend in service to the least of the earth or we will bend our knees to the kingdoms and powers of this world that so often contradict and stand in opposition to the kingdom of Jesus, the poor man crucified, the stranger, and the least at our door.

Let us pray. "Jesus, you are flesh of our flesh and bone of our bone and you bear the scars of violence and our inhumanity. You have known what it means to be human in all its dignity and its humiliation at the hands of others. And you dwell among us still, waiting for us to draw near to you and treat you with justice and mercy which make us all human, children of our Father. You are the Crucified One raised from the dead by the Father, and with the Spirit you will come again in glory one day to judge all the nations and each of us. Help us to live aware of the needs of others. Make us more and more human like you every day. Let us approach one another with respect, looking upon each other as you look upon us. May we so live as to find ourselves one day on your right side, hearing your words of blessing: 'Come, beloved of my Father! Come on home!' We ask this in your name, Jesus, the Son of Man. Amen."

THE FIFTH GLORIOUS MYSTERY:

The Trinity

SCRIPTURE

At that time Jesus was filled with the joy of the Holy Spirit and said, "I praise you, Father, Lord of heaven and earth, for you have hidden these things from the wise and learned, and made them known to the little ones. Yes, Father, such has been your gracious will. I have been given all things by my Father, so that no one knows the Son except the Father, and no one knows the Father except the Son and he to whom the Son chooses to reveal him." (Luke 10:21–22 and Matthew 11:25–27)

Or,

"I pray not only for these but also for those who through their word will believe in me. May they all be one as you Father are in me and I am in you. May they be one in us; so the world may believe that you have sent me.

"I have given them the Glory you have given me, that they may be one as we are one: I in them and you in me. Thus they shall reach perfection in unity and the world shall know that you have sent me and that I have loved them just as you loved me.

"Father, since you have given them to me I want them to be with me where I am and see the Glory you gave me, for you loved me before the foundation of the world.

"Righteous Father, the world has not known you but I have known you, and these have known that you have sent me. As I revealed your Name to them, so will I continue to reveal it, so that the love with which you loved me may be in them and I also may be in them." (John 17:20–26)

Or,

Then Jesus approached them and said, "I have been given all authority in heaven and on earth. Go, therefore, and make disciples from all nations. Baptize them in the Name of the Father and of the Son and of the Holy Spirit, and teach them to fulfill all that I have commanded you. I am with you always until the end of this world." (Matthew 28:18–20)

May the grace of our Lord Jesus Christ, the love of God and the fellowship of the Spirit be with you all.

—2 CORINTHIANS 13:13

In the opening chapter of John Paul II's Aspotolic Letter on the Rosary, he cites the stories of the

Transfiguration in the Gospels as an "icon of contemplation," and then goes on to look deeply into this icon and what it means for our faith.

> To look upon the face of Christ, to recognize its mystery amid the daily events and the sufferings of his human life, and then to grasp the divine splendor definitively revealed in the Risen Lord, seated in glory at the right hand of the Father: this is the task of every follower of Christ and therefore the task of each one of us. In contemplating Christ's face we become open to receiving the mystery of Trinitarian life, experiencing ever anew the love of the Father and delighting in the joy of the Holy Spirit. Saint Paul's words can then be applied to us: "Beholding the glory of the Lord, we are being changed into his likeness, from one degree of glory to another; for this comes from the Lord who is the Spirit." (2 Corinthians 3:18) (RVM, #9)

The mystery of our faith is the mystery of the Trinity. Divine revelation is self-revelation shared with all that God has created and sustains. God spoke one Word and that Word is the flesh of the Son of Man, Jesus the Lord. The Spirit came upon Jesus in its fullness. Jesus reveals humanly in his person and Word, his life, death, and resurrection, all that can be known of God in human terms. And Jesus' word for his human experience of God is Abba, "Father." The Prologue of John's gospel puts it this way:

And the Word was made flesh;
he had his tent pitched among us,
and we have seen his Glory,
the Glory of the only Son
coming from the Father:
fullness of truth and loving-kindness.
(John 1:14)

The rest of John's gospel tries to say that to believe in Jesus is to know the Father by the power of the Spirit, and that if we believe in Jesus then we must love as Jesus loves, by laying down our lives for one another, as Jesus has laid down his life for us. This is the love of God for us, known and experienced in Jesus. And the Spirit is the first gift given to those who believe so that we can experience this love and know the Father, as Jesus reveals him, as only Jesus can. This life that is everlasting begins in baptism and continues to deepen throughout our lives and after our deaths until the fullness of the resurrection of Jesus is shared with us. But to actually say anything about the mystery of the Trinity, about God, is daunting, and severely limited by our imaginations and language.

John Paul II calls the Trinity "the rhythm" of God's own life, the joyful communion of the Holy Trinity, our life's destiny and deepest longing." (RVM, #25) And our own human "rhythms" are meant to find their place and meaning in the all-encompassing rhythm of God. Sometimes our God is three and still our God is one. Our God is communion, unity, and diverse expression that is limitless. God always has more to say to us and is always seeking ways to express who he is to us. The God of the Israelites is Yahweh; the only God and his holiness were such that they did not even spell the name in its entirety or speak the name out loud. The images of this God abound in the books and psalms of the Old Testament.

> *I love you, O Lord, my strength.*
> *The Lord is my rock, my fortress,*
> *My deliverer and my God.*
> *He is the rock in whom I take refuge.*
> *He is my shield, my powerful savior, my stronghold.*
> *I call on the Lord, who is worthy of praise;*
> *He saves me from my enemies.*
> *(Psalm 18:2–4)*

The images are a litany of relationships: "the Lord is my shepherd" (Psalm 23); "O Lord my justice" (Psalm 4:2); "the Lord is a rampart for the oppressed; a refuge in times of distress" (Psalm 9:10); "the Lord is my light and salvation" (Psalm 27:1); "God is our strength and protection, an ever-present help in affliction . . . he puts an end to wars" (Psalm 46:2, 10). Some of the prayers reveal a depth of relationship and knowledge of God that question our own surety of how well we know God. The psalmist prays:

> God has spoken one word, and I have heard two things: that power belongs to God, and yours, O

God, is also mercy: you reward each one according to his deeds. (Psalm 62:12–13)

This God of power and might is also the God of tender regard, who loves his people as a father and mother
love their children, seeking always to draw us closer to his
presence. The people look for a home in God, as a spar-
row looks for a nest (Psalm 84:4). God is both justice that
bends down from the heavens to kiss faithfulness, and the
place where righteousness and peace embrace (Psalm 85).
This God loves the poor, the weak, the needy, and the afflicted while being a king that other nations serve (Psalm
72). This God of majesty and splendor, who has led his
people out of bondage into freedom and made a
covenant with them, has gone with them into exile when
they have strayed and broken the bonds of love and justice. This God is peace, mercy, and joy, trustworthy in a
world of injustice, evil, and death. This God is even described in terms of such vulnerability and tenderness:

I have quieted and stilled my soul
like a weaned child on its mother's lap;
like a contented child is my soul.
Hope in the Lord, O Israel, now and forever.
(Psalm 131:2–3)

This God is the Father, the God that Jesus knows intimately, being the Holy One of God, and it is this God
that Jesus reveals to all who listen and take to heart his

words, and put into practice the will of God. Only Jesus knows the Father and yet Jesus chooses to share intimacy and knowledge of the Father with us. The gift of the Spirit is Jesus' breath and life force given to us so that we can call God our Father with Jesus and come to know God ever more deeply. Our God is a community and we are invited into that communion, to dwell in God. We are invited to dwell with one another as God is three and God is one.

This is the root of our very existence. This union of persons has nothing to do, in a sense, with male or female images, but with relationships. The English mystic Julian of Norwich, in the fourteenth century, wrote in her *Showing,* "the deep wisdom of the Trinity is our mother, in whom we are enclosed." Our God is the loving Father who received Jesus' broken, dying spirit as he cried out on the cross. Then, raised from the dead by the Father, Jesus greets his friends with the cry of "Shalom— Peace." Our God is Peace. The mystery of our God resists easy description, facile explanations, and familiar creedal statements that can serve as a jumping-off place for prayer, contemplation, and knowledge of God that is only learned from God: Father, Son and Spirit.

We are made in this image of God. Not only in the image of male and female, as first revealed in Genesis; we are made in the image of the Trinity, and, in community we are made human, whole, and holy. John F. X. Harriott wrote this piece almost fifteen years ago, called "Periscope, Faith's Central Mystery," in *The Tablet,* January 14, 1989.

If we are made in the image of God, we are made in the image of the Trinity; and the life of the Trinity must in some sort be reflected in the pattern of our human life . . . Thus to the Father is credited all that we understand by generation, creation, maintenance; and much of our human activity can be seen as cooperation in that work . . . Likewise, all human works of compassion, healing, reconciliation, sacrifice, forgiveness, making amends and making good again reflect the work of redemption and reconciliation identified most closely with the Son . . . And finally the special role of the Holy Spirit is reflected in every positive idea and inspiration, however slight and humble, in every advance in knowledge and wisdom, in every flash of imagination, in every movement of the heart.

These are distinctions and divisions of the work of God in differing persons that are in communion with one another: a way to speak about the work of God in our lives, the world, and history. But the work of one is the work of all. They are one. The love of God, the Father, Son, and Spirit, are all found in the cross, forgiveness and salvation that is shared among us—there are no distinctions among them. We are caught grasping at expressions to seek understanding. In the mystery of the Incarnation, the communion of God now penetrates all of human life, human persons, and political, economic, and social situations. The God of history is also the God of intimate detail, of singularity and awesome universality. The heart of the matter is that we only live in this God and God lives in us, each and all of us, and so our ultimate destiny is communion, with each other, with God and in God, and through the power and mercy of God. We stumble as we search for the words.

The Carmelite mystic John of the Cross wrote a poem-prayer "The Holy Trinity." Here are selections from it, using another vocabulary to express some inkling of who our God is and what God is to us.

> *As the love in the beloved*
> *Each lived in the other,*
> *And the Love that unites them*
> *Is one with them,*
>
> *Their equal, excellent as*
> *The One and the Other:*
> *Three Persons, and one Beloved*
> *Among all three.*
>
> *One love in them all*
> *Makes of them one Lover,*
> *And the Lover is the Beloved*
> *In whom each one lives.*
>
> *. . . Thus it is a boundless*
> *Love that unites them,*
> *For the three have one love*

Which is their essence;
And the more love is one
The more it is love.

Throughout history since the Incarnation, knowledge about the Trinity has been learned first through prayer, as the Spirit teaches anyone who stands in the presence of God. The Trinity holds us, encompasses us, dwells within us, and no matter who we are and where we are, we are in God, as the Father, the Son, and the Spirit are in one another. Ritually in prayer we talk about praying to the Father, with the Son, and in the Spirit (the Doxology of the Eucharist). We know God-Father by the gift of the Spirit in the incarnated person of Jesus. All of these statements say something and we can be totally unaware of any or all of it. Yet prayer, worship, and a life of faith exist to draw us ever more deeply into this life of the Trinity and drive us to express this life in the way we relate to one another in the world. To be "Trinitarian" we must think and live and relate in terms of community, of unity and diversity, of mutuality and love, of communication and freedom, of being so interconnected that we do not make sense without the other, without all others. The mystery of the Trinity is bound so closely to that of the Incarnation and the cross. We are made in the image of God and we are made in the image of the cross. Our relationship with God is only as true and holy as our relationship with others, and for those who believe in Jesus as Lord, our relation to God is only as holy as our relationship to our enemies.

When the Father raises Jesus from the dead and he returns to his disciples and community, the first word to them and to us is *Shalom—Peace.* Jesus is the Word made flesh. Jesus is *Peace* made flesh. And as he shows them his hands and side, his scars of love, his words and wounds are breath that is the Spirit poured out on us. Father, Jesus, and Spirit are one and we are drawn into this Trinity through our baptisms. We dwell in God, in the body of Christ, in community, in the Spirit that stirs us to pray in terms that are always plural and universal: our Father, our Lord, our Life, our Spirit, our God. Our God draws us outside and beyond ourselves into others, bursting what appears to be isolation and individuality that shrink our ability to love, to forgive, to obey, and to do justice and be at peace with each other.

At the end of each decade of the Rosary and reflection upon a mystery, we say the Doxology, the short prayer that addresses God as Trinity: "Glory be to the Father and to the Son and to the Holy Spirit, as it was in the beginning, is now and will be forever. Amen." This says it all, and yet what it says can only be learned in the Trinity, only spoken in the Spirit, only seen through Jesus, and only known in the Father. Being in the presence of God, beyond words, concepts, desires, and images, brings us to awareness and relationships that are truer than any expression of words. We pray to live. We live to worship. We worship the Trinity and in God we become human: we become community and we dwell in communion with God, who is Three and who is One. We dwell in that place where they are Three yet One, where they are Love.

Let us pray. "Father, you have spoken your Word. Jesus and your beloved is flesh, human with us. Jesus, you have prayed that we might know the Father who sent you to us. Spirit, you have been given to us in the breath of Jesus to be our courage and our truth and your compelling force for peace in the world. Holy Ones, make us holy as you are and draw us ever more deeper into your dwelling place. May we always remember that there is room in you for all of us and that we are made in your image. May we reveal that image to all the world by working for unity, communion, and peace on earth and living together in your Love. We bless you, O Holy Trinity. Amen."

Closing Story

At the beginning of the Gulf War in 1990, a young Iraqi soldier told me this story and it has overshadowed my life ever since. It is about prayer, and sideways, so to speak, it is about Myriam, Mary of Nazareth.

Once upon a time there was a devout Muslim. He made it a point never to miss the prayers. Five times a day, no matter what he was doing, he was aware that he must stop everything immediately as soon as he heard the summons from the pinnacle of the minarets. He was also a very shrewd businessman, wealthy, and gave generously, as the Koran commands, to the poor. One day he was in his shop and about to make one of the biggest sales of the year, if not ever in his life. A merchant was poring over twenty or more fine carpets, intending to buy them for his house and as a donation to a study hall and side rooms in his hometown mosque. Huge carpets lay strewn over every space and draped over tables and chairs. He chose one, then another, but he was taking his time, selecting only what he considered the best for his purchases. And the other merchant himself became aware that soon the call for prayers would intrude on the sale. He began to hurry the man along in his decisions, but he would have none of it.

The call was sounded and the buyer either didn't hear it or ignored it. The merchant became frantic, pushing prayer rugs and carpets on him. "Here, take this one," he said and threw it over the shoulders of one of the man's servants. "Here, this one also. Take it home, sit on it, pray on it, or eat on it. Decide whether or not you like it or if it is suitable for your needs. Come back tomorrow and we will make a good deal." It seemed to take forever before he got the man out the door and he closed the shop to go to the mosque. He knew he was late, very late for the prayers, but he might get there for some of them.

He ran out the door and into a huge crowd. Where did all these people come from today? He pushed through, down one side street, only to find his way blocked, turned around and back into the larger street. Finally he got back to his shop and ran out the back door, and took any street that looked deserted and ran for the mosque. Then he ran into a beggar, a very aggressive one. He had no money! He had left it in his shop in his haste. Finally, he took off his vest and shoes and nearly threw them at the beggar trying to tear himself loose and ran for the mosque.

He finally arrived, gasping for breath, and stopped, dismayed. The last of those praying were leaving, taking their shoes and returning to their homes and shops. He was brokenhearted. He had never missed prayers in his adult life. The man who attended to the shoes looked up at him, when he heard this great sigh come forth from him in disappointment. The merchant said: "The prayers are over: I missed them?"

"Yes," the attendant answered, "and we started late today, which is very unusual . . . as though we were waiting for someone."

Dejectedly the man turned to walk away but he was stopped by the attendant. "Look," he said, "I know you are disappointed that you missed prayers. How about we make a deal?"

"What? What do you mean?"

"Why, in our tradition," the man said, "I can trade you my prayers from this service and all their merit for . . . say, your sigh that you missed them."

"You would do that," the merchant asked.

"Sure," he said. "I never miss the prayers. I collect the shoes, watch them, sit at the back, and pray."

The merchant was relieved. This was the perfect antidote to his sorrow. "Done!" They bowed to one another and the prayers and merit changed lives. And the merchant went home, feeling relieved.

That night, however, he had a dream. The Angel Gabriel appeared at the foot of his bed with enormous wings spread in light and colors that defied description, towering twenty feet above him, looking down on him, his face sad and his head moving from side to side. "What? Am I dying? Did I do something wrong?" The merchant sat bolt up in the bed facing the angel. "Why do you look at me and shake your head like that?"

Gabriel answered him, "Bad deal. Bad deal. Terribly bad deal."

"What? Why?"

Gabriel went on: "God was so pleased with your sigh. That was a pure prayer. And your sigh was worth more to God than every prayer that man ever said in his life! Bad deal." Then the man woke up with a start, wondering about the dream.

When the story was finished the young Iraqi soldier looked at me expectantly. And then he asked if I knew about the prayer of the sigh. I stumbled, and mumbled, "Uh, I do not know, but I think I do." He told me then that to pray without words, without thoughts, without desire, only with intent on worshiping and pleasing God, is the most powerful prayer, the only one we need to learn. And then he said: "It is the way the holy ones pray, like your Mary, who we call Myriam, the mother of Jesus, the messenger of God. She does not pray in words. She sighs. She sighs a lot when she sees what people do to each other, and Allah hears her sighs and they mean more than any other prayers." I do not know if that is a tradition in Islam, among Muslims, but it rings true.

Mary prays and sighs. The breath of the Spirit of God that came upon her, when the power of the Most High overshadowed her at the moment of the Incarnation, when the Word of God leapt down into her womb and her heart, is released and sent forth into the world, upon the world. These are the only prayers that are heard over all the entreaties and requests. It is pure prayer born of obedience to the will of God and sorrow that the Word of God is rejected, with consequences of violence and evil let loose in the world.

As the young soldier walked away from me, he turned and said, "I hope you will pray that way, learning to sigh over what your people, Christians, and your country does to us. She must look at you in sorrow and be forever sighing." I said nothing: What was there to say? It is true. Myriam, who is a disciple of her son, Jesus, who follows him so closely, must dwell in sorrow over the state of the children of God on earth today. May we all stop and pray, with Mary, with all the disciples of the Word of God made flesh, and sigh, believing that the Spirit of God in us will bring the rain-rein-reign of justice and peace upon the earth, to the glory of God the Father. We sigh, and pray in the name of our Father, the Son, and the Holy Spirit. Amen.

INDEX